KATE

KATE

A Biography

MARCIA MOODY

Michael O'Mara Books Limited

This book is for all those who
have been inspired by Kate.

First published in Great Britain in 2013 by
Michael O'Mara Books Limited
9 Lion Yard
Tremadoc Road
London SW4 7NQ

A CIP catalogue record for this book is available from the British Library.

Papers used by Michael O'Mara Books Limited are natural, recyclable products
made from wood grown in sustainable forests. The manufacturing processes
conform to the environmental regulations of the country of origin.

ISBN: 978-1-78243-109-1 in hardback print format
ISBN: 978-1-78243-171-8 in trade paperback format
ISBN: 978-1-78243-113-8 in Epub format
ISBN: 978-1-78243-112-1 in Mobipocket format

3 4 5 6 7 8 9 10

Designed by Ana Bjezancevic

Printed and bound by CPI Group (UK) Ltd, Croydon, CR0 4YY

www.mombooks.com

CONTENTS

Introduction

Catherine Elizabeth Middleton, Kate, Waity Kaitie, Sizzler Sister, the Duchess of Cambridge, the High Street Duchess. The woman who has held all of these titles is fonder of some than of others, but it is important to remember that, over the years, each of these names has been bestowed on her by someone else. Because she is a naturally private person, others have often projected an image onto her, associated with one of these names, which is completely at odds with who she really is. Underneath, she has remained the same person throughout, and that person remains something of an enigma.

For over ten years she has been the person closest to the man who will one day be king, but she only slowly slipped into the public's consciousness, like the royal family's stealth missile. When she and Prince William first met, in 2001, his family had just come through a decade of divorce, mud-slinging and changing public opinion. There had been questions raised as to the significance of a monarchy in the modern age, while after years behind palace walls the Princess of Wales and Duchess of York had publicly criticized many aspects of the institution. It became clear that there had been a disconnection between the royals and their public. As with everything in life, constant small adaptations were required in order to ensure continued success, and while things imploded in the nineties, the 2000s were about mending and about making those changes.

When William first started university an agreement was made between the palace and the press that he would be left to study in peace in exchange for regular interviews and photocalls. This meant that Kate was able to enter the prince's life unnoticed at first, while they worked out how they felt about each other – a luxury unheard of for previous generations of royals.

She was by William's side for eight years before they got engaged, and although their brief breakup made the headlines, for the most part over the years she was a low-key public presence. It was only when their engagement was announced that the spotlight was shone squarely on her and she became one of the most famous women in the world. By this time she had become a valuable asset to the royal family. She was stable, intelligent, charming, strong and confident. She had been there for William when he was unhappy at university, dealing with family bereavements and messy public court cases, and coming to terms with what lay ahead for him in the future.

In turn, he had been there for her through her own family bereavements and had given her support and invaluable first-hand advice to help her to come to terms with becoming a public figure. She got on well with his family, and he with hers, and most importantly they were in love. They made each other laugh, they looked after each other and they were a good match.

Until their engagement, Kate had always been viewed by the public as an extension of William, which she appreciated and understood, as he was the one who had been born into royalty and a life in the spotlight. She came into his life when he was coming of age and learning about his role, and Kate supported him through that time while continuing to study and then to work. While there would always be certain demands on the partner of a member of the royal family, Kate wasn't required to invest so much time and energy on supporting hers because she was a woman. When Prince Philip married the Queen, he gave up a promising naval career, but has managed to combine his support of her with successfully carving his own path.

Kate has become more than just her husband's wife, and is forging ahead into the future, impressing all those she works with, thanks to her scrupulous attention to detail, her natural warmth, empathy and dedication. Even before she entered royal life, she was drawn to the support of vulnerable children and has also shown that she is willing to confront the more 'raw, ugly, dirty and difficult' issues such as addiction. For their wedding day, she and William wrote a prayer that they recited in their vows, which included the line, 'Help us serve and comfort those who suffer', and with this pledge it is clear how they see their role in the future of the royal family. Kate's mother, Carole, raised three children while building her own business from scratch, and Kate intends to follow in her footsteps, combining motherhood with her public duties.

Now Kate is a senior member of the royal family and on the brink of motherhood, it is time to look at the woman behind the name. She is the first person for 350 years without aristocratic blood to marry an heir to the throne, and if it wasn't for tragedy on both sides of her family, she would probably not be in the position she is today. However, circumstances before she was born and the support her parents gave her only got her so far – the rest has been up to her.

Although she was christened Catherine, she started to be called Kate at university and Kate is what William calls her. It became how she was referred to in the press, and therefore how she is known all around the world, and so that is how she will be referred to in this book. One day she will be Queen Catherine, but for now, she is known and loved as Kate ...

CHAPTER ONE

A tragic turn of events

The British winter of 1982 was bitterly cold, and in the January an unrelenting blizzard swept across the country. Hundreds of roads were closed, trains were cancelled and schools were shut. The country was in chaos. But while the police were advising people to stay home, Carole and Michael Middleton were making a treacherous journey to their local hospital as Carole was about to give birth to their first child. The attractive but unassuming young couple had been married for a year and a half, worked hard and were liked by their neighbours. They both came from close families, and were overjoyed when their healthy baby girl finally came into the world. Catherine Elizabeth Middleton was born at the Royal Berkshire Hospital in Reading on Saturday, 9 January 1982. She was a bonnie baby with a mop of dark hair, and was soon bundled in blankets and brought home to her parents' modest house deep in the Berkshire countryside.

Although the newborn was blissfully unaware, this triumph in the face of adversity was the culmination of a much longer journey. It was a journey that not only her mother Carole had made, but Carole's ancestors before her. For over a century, her mother's maternal ancestors, the Harrisons, worked down the coal mines, six days a week, eighteen hours a day, facing potential death on a daily basis – whether from fires and explosions, or being crushed by trams. Diseases such as tuberculosis, cholera and polio ripped through the poverty-stricken villages, leaving orphans, widows and grief-stricken parents to try to come to terms with their losses. The Harrisons lived in County Durham, just south of Newcastle, and worked in the pits owned by the Bowes-Lyons, the Queen Mother's family. Who knows how long this pattern of sons following their fathers down the mines would have continued, were it not for a heartbreaking loss for one young boy. Thomas Harrison, the boy who was to become Kate's great-grandfather, lost his own father during the First World War when he was aged just fourteen. However, while it was a painful bereavement, it changed not only his life, but the lives if his descendants forever. It meant that he broke away from his mining ancestry, and went to work for his maternal grandfather who was a carpenter. He married and had a daughter Dorothy – Kate's grandmother – and when the country began to put itself back together after the Second World War, the family moved south in search of better fortunes.

They settled in Southall, located in the outer sprawl of London, and this is where Dorothy later met and fell in love with Ron Goldsmith – Kate's grandfather. Although the Goldsmiths hadn't experienced the lowest-rung occupation of mining, they were still dirt-poor, working as labourers and mechanics. They were originally from Kent and, it is said, mixed with criminals, some of whom were deported to Australia. However, it was Kate's great-great-grandfather John Goldsmith who changed their fortunes by moving first to London and then to Southall to follow the work. Two generations later, when Kate's grandparents met, Dorothy was working in high street clothing store Dorothy Perkins and Ron for a haulage company. Dorothy had aspirations to better herself and the drive to help her achieve it – the less complimentary in Ron's family described her as pushy, with airs and graces, but others considered her a charming and popular woman.

'Dorothy had a lovely manner about her,' remembers Dudley Singleton, who knew Dorothy and Ron later, when they lived in the same village. 'She had a way of walking which was natural to her – very upright. She was always smiling and had what was interpreted as a rather regal manner, hence her nickname 'The Duchess'. She and Ron were very well-liked. He was a quiet man with a ready smile.' The couple were in love and, after they married, they lived with his widowed mother before moving into a council flat nearby. They then eventually borrowed the money from Ron's brother-in-law to buy their first home, and this was to become the first home of their daughter, Carole Elizabeth Goldsmith, who was born on 31 January 1955.

Carole was an only child for nine years before her brother Gary was born, and soon after that the family moved to nearby Norwood Green – a significant change from the impoverished Southall, but still not an affluent area. Although they had their own place, it was in the middle of a council estate, built on a piece of land that had been bombed in the war. However, it was theirs and, rather than buy a small place they could easily afford, they made the decision to invest in a bigger home, which they would then make sure they could afford. Ron had worked hard as a lorry driver, taking on extra shifts in order to better the fortunes of his family, while Dorothy stayed home with their children when they were young, and worked for an estate agent in between. After the move, Ron set up his own building company, and worked hard to make a success of that too. The children thrived.

Blonde-haired Carole played in her school's brass band and was known at the time as a girlie girl; she liked wearing pink and dancing in front of the TV during *Top of the Pops*, and she was very close to her baby brother Gary. When she was a teenager she started listening to soul music, some of her favourite artists being Stevie Wonder and Earth, Wind and Fire. She worked at clothing store C&A, and was seen as an effortless beauty.

'Carole wasn't a girl for makeup,' her cousin Ann Terry told Claudia Joseph for her book *Kate Middleton: Princess in Waiting*. 'She was a very natural girl who was happy in jeans and a sloppy jumper, more of a country girl. But she was very pretty.' It wasn't until Carole was twenty-one and started working for British Airways, where she met a dashing young co-worker called Michael Middleton, that her own life changed significantly.

The Middletons' fortunes had been much more bountiful than that of the Goldsmiths and the Harrisons. They were made up of five generations of wealthy Leeds solicitors. Additionally, Kate's great-grandfather Noel Middleton had married society beauty Olive Lupton, who was the daughter of a wealthy mill owner, Francis Lupton, and it is from this man that Kate's father's side of the family predominantly inherited their wealth. Francis Lupton had three sons and two daughters, but tragically all three of his sons were killed in the First World War, and their heartbroken father never recovered. These losses meant that his two daughters inherited his vast wealth, rather than it being distributed through the five siblings. When Francis died, Olive inherited what would today be worth around £10 million.

Through the Luptons, Kate is distantly related to Prince William, as they are both descended from the English Civil War parliamentarian Sir Thomas Fairfax – William through his mother's side, and Kate on her father's side, meaning the couple are fifteenth cousins. However, it is also worth noting that the similarly unaristocratic Sophie, Countess of Wessex, who was the daughter of a tyre salesman and a secretary, is also distantly related to her husband, Prince Edward, as they are eleventh cousins once removed. It seems that many other 'commoners' would find they have royal connections if they traced their ancestry back far enough.

Noel and Olive had two sons, Kate's grandfather Peter and his brother Anthony, and when they were grown, within a year they had married twin sisters Valerie and Mary Glassborow. The girls were from the East End of London, but raised in Marseilles, and descended from a line of clerks and bankers. Kate's grandfather Peter broke the Middleton family's line of solicitors by training in the RAF and, after the Second World War, he went to work as a pilot for British European Airways (which later became British Airways). It was a profession that would influence his second son Michael's career choice decades later. During the war, Peter flew a mosquito fighter-bomber and his aim was to try to tip the wings of German flying bombs to make them crash in the relative safety of the English countryside, rather than on their target of London.

The second of four sons, Michael Francis Middleton was

born on 23 June 1949. Three years later the family moved to Buckinghamshire to be near Peter's new work for BEA at Heathrow. It was in this capacity that Peter accompanied the Duke of Edinburgh on a two-week tour of South America. Peter was selected by his employers to act as First Officer, often flying with the Duke, and later received a letter and a pair of gold cufflinks from Buckingham Palace as a sign of appreciation.

Michael Middleton went away to Clifton College boarding school in Bristol, and initially dreamed of becoming a pilot like this father. BEA joined with British Overseas Airways Corporation in 1972 to become British Airways, and Michael started working for the company, based at Heathrow Airport as a flight dispatcher. He wore a uniform of navy-blue trousers and jacket with gold bands around the arms, to denote how long he had been with the company, teamed with a white shirt, navy tie and red hat. He and his fellow dispatchers were known in the industry as 'red caps' and their jobs depended on their efficiency. Michael was responsible for coordinating the aircraft on the ground between arrival and departure. Before take-off he would be on the craft, supervising the loading of the plane to make sure the correct food and fuel was taken on, and that the correct number of passengers were on board compared to check-in, so that the plane was allowed to take off. When a plane landed at Heathrow, he would also be the first on board to exchange technical notes with the pilot, before moving on to the cabin crew to check on housekeeping details. It was in this way that the dark, handsome and unassuming Michael first met a vivacious young stewardess called Carole Goldsmith.

Air travel in the 1960s and early 70s was the ultimate in high-flying glamour. It was a luxury only a few could afford, so working as one of the cabin crew was a prestigious job. Stewardesses had to be bubbly, attractive and young, and those who put on a few pounds were taken aside for a quiet word. By the time Carole Goldsmith started at the age of twenty-one, in 1976, the times had changed a little, as package holidays were being introduced and air travel was slightly more accessible. Planes were getting bigger and faster so cabin crews were getting larger, but it was still a very sought-after job, with an unforgivingly rigorous admission process. Before training began, Carole had to be successful in a strict interview, where she was scored according to how she gelled with the interviewer, her use of eye contact, the way she dressed, the way she sat in her chair and how she spoke. Her prospective employers would not have marked someone down if they had an accent, but they were looking for people who didn't use slang words or cut their words short. Their speech needed to be clear and distinctive.

Once Carole had passed her interview she embarked on six weeks of training, which covered a multitude of areas. One member of staff responsible for training new cabin crew in the period Carole was starting out explains, 'Hair had to be short or worn up – not on the collar of the blouse. Female cabin crew had to wear a certain type of lipstick and they were shown how to do their makeup by professional people. Nails had to be clean and well manicured. Tights had to be a certain colour, and shoes polished and not down at the heel. Hats and gloves had to be worn at all times when in uniform.'

The prospective crew members all went through their paces at the training school at Cranebank, which was affectionately known as 'the college of knowledge'. There Carole was taught how to serve customers in a professional manner, and mix a selection of cocktails including a classic champagne cocktail, martini, gimlet and Bloody Mary. There were mocked-up aircrafts with existing BA crew acting as customers so the trainees could practise serving. All trainees were also taught deportment by walking down a catwalk, and given assistance to be good listeners, have good eye contact and always have a smile on their face when dealing with customers. The former trainer recalls, 'You were tested on all elements you had been taught, and you had to obtain a certain pass mark.'

Carole's brother Gary recalls, 'I remember her training. She used to practise doing her announcements and record them onto a tape recorder, much to my amusement.'

Many commented on how composed the Middletons were at the royal wedding and, however much that came naturally, it seems likely that at least some of Carole's early BA training set her in good stead for many areas of her life that were to follow. At the time, her training was almost like an antiquated and condensed finishing school, but now it simply comes across as old-fashioned good manners and poise. The same qualities can also be seen in Kate herself, in the way she carries herself, always with a smile on her face, well-put-together, sociable and with impeccable manners.

Safety training for Carole and her colleagues involved time in swimming pools learning how to inflate life rafts, put life jackets on passengers and work the emergency chutes. They also learned first aid, which included how to deliver a baby, CPR, knowing how to administer the drugs carried on the aircraft for different passengers, being able to treat wounds, put an arm in a sling and treat a broken leg. The pass mark for safety and first aid was ninety-eight per cent, and if trainees didn't pass first time around they could try again, but if they failed a second time they were out of the company.

Once Carole had passed in all areas, she was ready to start her globetrotting new career. She was fully equipped to deliver a baby, mix a martini and save a life – all with a smile on her face and no ladders in her tights. The BA uniform in the seventies was still very proper and traditional. Her uniform was made up of a white blouse with wide A-line collar, worn underneath a long fitted navy jacket buttoned right down the front, a mid-calf-length navy skirt, navy hat and matching gloves. Life as a cabin crew member was very different from her previous working life, and she had to adapt quickly. She might spend up to twenty-one days away from home, and had to be prepared for day or night flights, working long hours and sleeping at odd times. When she went home she was catching up on time zones and missed sleep. But it was an exciting life and – depending on the length of the flight – she would sometimes have two or three days at the other end of a trip overseas to acclimatize.

For a twenty-one-year-old it was quite a life to suddenly be a part of. The social scene between crew members overseas was fun, and they were given foreign currency for living expenses while they were away. In 1976, air travel was a different world. Some male holidaymakers, who were just getting used to the etiquette, would walk up the steps on to the plane bare-chested or even still wearing their swimming trunks at the end of their holiday, although most pilots would insist they turn around and get changed before they were permitted to board. It was also in the days when smoking was commonplace on aircraft, and one former crew member recalls that the cabin crew would all be smoking in the little galley kitchen when they weren't tending to the customers, and they would emerge with their serving trays in a fug of smoke. There were many romances between staff – cabin crew would marry cabin crew, some would marry pilots. As Carole Goldsmith and Michael Middleton shared early pleasantries at work it became clear that they shared a chemistry and, before long, they were a couple. It was a busy time for them both, and they worked hard – although they both worked unusual hours, they each understood that was just the way it was for now. Like all other staff members, they were given a number of free flights a year, as well as having access to other flights which could be purchased for just ten per cent of the original price.

The fledgling couple hadn't been together long when they decided to move in together in nearby Slough, an industrial suburb situated conveniently close to Heathrow. Although living together before marriage was a very 'modern' move, they clearly knew where their future lay, and became engaged in 1979. Around the same time they bought their first home, on Cock Lane, in the village of Bradfield, Berkshire, for £34,000. The red-brick semi-detached house named West View was cosy and modest, nestled in a typically English leafy country lane, with the village hall, local pub and primary school nearby. Local estate agent Dudley Singleton knew them both and remembered, 'Carole was a very stylish lady – gregarious and smiling with a good personality, and Michael was quiet and reserved, sensible, strong and easy-going.'

They married on 21 June 1980, in the nearby church of St James the Less. Unlike her daughter over thirty years later, Carole arrived in a horse and carriage – thanks to her mother Dorothy's drive and charm, and her father Ron's talent and hard work, her family had already come a long way from their council-flat roots in Southall. The reception was held in nearby Tudor manor house Dorney Court, with champagne and canapés, before the family moved on to Michael's brother Simon's house for chilli and a party.

Carole became pregnant the following spring, and gave up Heathrow for the hedgerows of Berkshire for good, deciding to take a £5,000 redundancy package from BA. Instead, she was to focus on a blossoming business idea that would later make her and her husband millionaires. But, for now, the Middletons were focused on their new addition.

On the day that Kate was born, the country was freezing and struggling to function – covered in a blanket of snow. In fact, January 1982 was the coldest month ever on record for Berkshire. After being brought home from the hospital, Kate settled in and was a good-natured baby. Carole was a natural mother, quickly establishing a routine with regular eating and sleeping times. There were other like-minded young mums in the area and Carole made friends easily. One neighbour, George Brown, gave birth to her daughter Nicola just four days after Carole had Kate and recalls, 'Carole and I would take the girls out for walks together and have a coffee and there was never much crying. Catherine was a good baby.'

Five-month-old Kate was christened at St Andrew's, Bradfield, on 20 June that year, and her little family were reminiscent of families up and down the country, with Michael in a smart suit, Carole in a floral dress and Kate wearing a traditional white christening gown. The following day, Prince William was born. The Middletons would have taken at least a casual interest in the birth of the future king, as not only was the Princess of Wales's first pregnancy announced while Carole was expecting her own first-born, but the royal family were at that time enjoying a golden era in the eyes of their public. The young Diana was the particular favourite and her wedding to the Prince of Wales the year before was a cause for massive celebration. The news that Princess Diana was then expecting their first-born was greeted with countrywide excitement. Magazine covers bloomed with pictures of the pregnant princess, and boasted information about her maternity style. It wasn't until more than a decade later it became public knowledge that Diana's pregnancy with William was fraught with terrible anxiety, and it was in the month that Kate was born that Diana threw herself down the stairs at Sandringham in a plea for help. But, at the time, she was smiling for the cameras, and women all over the world followed her every move, copying her hairstyle and emulating her wardrobe. This is the image of the princess that Carole would have seen on the newsstands and TV screens.

Carole showed signs that she had a keen sense of occasion. She convinced her friend George Brown of the importance of marking children's birthdays – even if the child was just a year old. As a mum of three, George wasn't going to throw a party for her youngest who was turning one, but she recalls that Carole said she must mark the milestone and brought Kate over to celebrate with hats and cake. By this time, Carole was pregnant again, and she gave birth to her second daughter Philippa Charlotte Middleton on 6 September 1983, although the dark-haired little girl was soon referred to as Pippa. Life continued as normal, and Kate attended the local playgroup at St Peter's Church Hall. But Carole and Michael soon had a decision to make.

In the first few years of Kate's life, Britain was bruised and broken. There had been countrywide riots the year before, and in Carole's old turf of Southall, 120 people were injured in a clash between racist skinheads and Asian youths in the same pub in which Carole's parents had celebrated their wedding reception.

There was public uproar about the Conservative government's cuts to public spending, while unemployment was the highest it had been since before the Second World War. In April 1981, the Falklands War raged for over two months, and IRA bombs had killed many in the years before and after her birth.

Although there was some money coming in from Michael's side of the family, the Middletons were on a single wage, and when the idea of living and working overseas came up, Carole and Michael decided to go for it. Lots of BA staff took similar offers by which they and their families would be sent all over the world to live in a different country for a few years. For the Middletons, their new home was to be Jordan in the Middle East – a small country that shares borders with Israel, Syria, Iraq and Saudi Arabia. It was a bold decision for a young couple with a two-year-old and an eight-month-old to uproot to a place thousands of miles away where they had no family or friends. They would be moving from their tiny leafy village to the hilly wild terrain of Amman, in the northern part of Jordan. However, it was a good time for them to go – neither girl was old enough to go to school and so there was no routine to disrupt, and they would move back to the UK just in time for Kate to start school. Plus, it was a good chance to try something different, enjoy the sun and make some money. It was only a five-hour flight, with a two-hour time difference, so they would easily be able to take trips back home.

In May 1984, the family of four flew east into the sun. They were following in the footsteps of Carole's father, Ron, who had been stationed out there on National Service as a teenager but, while both were used to foreign travel from their work at BA, it was the first time Carole and Michael had lived overseas themselves

– and it was a completely different world to what they were used to. Amman was a bustling, dusty and thriving city full of souks, mosques and street traders. There were horses and donkeys in the streets, and the people lived in typically Arabian square white houses with flat roofs. The food was predominantly Lebanese, which meant lots of stuffed vine leaves, rice, lamb and flatbreads, along with plenty of fresh fruit and vegetables. As a ninety per cent Muslim country, the air often undulated with sounds of the call to prayer from the minaret towers. The family needed to get used to English not being the first language, the currency of Jordanian dinars and the different national holidays of Eid Mubarak and Ramadan, instead of Christmas and Easter. In Jordan, Friday, not Sunday, was the day of rest and people worked at weekends.

The young family moved into in a simple one-storey, flat-roofed building in the shadow of a tower block. The rent was paid for by BA, which meant they could keep their Berkshire home to return to. Michael worked at the Queen Alia International Airport, which had only opened the previous year. He worked this time as a station manager, with a team of people beneath him. He drove a company car and played tennis at the British Embassy. BA provided the family with free flights back home, and sometimes Carole and the girls would go back home together for a few days, leaving Michael in Jordan. The family would return home together for Christmas too, but they also made the most of their surroundings.

As a family, the Middletons have always enjoyed being outdoors and they explored the country while they were there, visiting local sites such as the Greco-Roman ruins in Jerash. Their own area was dusty and rocky and full of orange and olive trees; however, they could also venture down to the Jordan River, which separated the country from Israel, and cut through a lush, picturesque valley. At home, they would eat out on their veranda and, before long, Kate and Pippa's hair went golden blonde in the sun. Kate helped to personalize her new bedroom by putting Mickey Mouse stickers on her wardrobe door and she attended the Al Saheera nursery, where she learned nursery rhymes in Arabic. To the amusement of those around her, was able to sing 'Happy Birthday' in Arabic before she could sing it in English.

However, as much as the Middletons enjoyed their exotic sojourn, before long it was time to return home ...

CHAPTER TWO

A girl called Squeak

There were frequent trips back to Berkshire, but not long after Kate's fourth birthday, the family were up in the air again – and this time they were going home for good. Nestled down a country lane lined with oaks and bracken, West View had been the first house Kate had ever lived in, but it was only now that she was old enough to be aware of it. Crunching up the short gravel drive, going into the red-brick house with the scarlet front door and sleeping in her snug little bedroom all came to mean home to her. Her first bedroom in the house was a tiny sliver of a room under the eaves, with a steeply sloping ceiling and slanted window. All of the rooms were small and cosy, but the girls also had the run of the spacious garden, which had lots of trees and featured their own Wendy house.

There wasn't much time to get used to the change of home, because Kate was also starting a new school. Instead of going to the local junior school, which was a one-minute walk round the corner, she was enrolled in the private St Andrew's, Pangbourne, a ten-minute drive away. Inheritance on the Middleton side and money saved during their two years in Jordan meant that the £4,000-a-term fees were covered, and once the four-year-old Kate was decked out in her brand-new white shirt, black tie, green jumper, green blazer and blue kilt, she was ready to go.

Set down a long and winding driveway amidst fifty-four acres of woodland, St Andrew's was the dream environment for the young Kate and played a large part in shaping the woman she has become. The main buildings were set around a Victorian mansion, but the school had up-to-the-minute facilities and numerous playing fields, of which Kate would make full use during her time there. Carole and Michael had already instilled manners and discipline in their children, but one of the aims of St Andrew's was to build on this kind of social conduct. The school was at the forefront of a new kind of education, striving for excellence in the traditional areas of academia, sports and the arts, but also focusing on producing well-rounded, community-minded children. In fact, the school states its values as 'respect, kindness, politeness, teamwork, honesty, enthusiasm and perseverance'. It was a Church of England school, and so there was also chapel every week and Christian holidays were celebrated with special services.

The family adjusted to life back in the countryside and Carole, who was pregnant for the third time, started providing treats and toys for local children's parties. Chatting with the other mums, she had felt there was a lack of reasonably priced party wear available. After doing some research, Carole started filling that hole in the market – firstly with the people she knew locally, selling party bags in the village hall, but quickly venturing further afield.

Carole and Michael's first and only son, James William Middleton, was born on 15 April 1987, shortly after Kate had turned five. His big sisters doted on him, and still do. 'They look after him like their little precious,' their uncle Gary Goldsmith later recalled. However, the birth of her third child didn't slow Carole down. While Kate found her feet at school, Carole was on a roll with her new venture. The same year as baby James was born, so also was her business, Party Pieces, which started out as a mail-order company. Carole photographed her first catalogue using Kate and Pippa as models. The sisters were dressed up in T-shirts with their ages on them and held cupcakes.

The quaint and unassuming little corner of the Berkshire countryside was the perfect environment for Kate and her siblings to thrive. Bradfield was a tiny village where everyone knew each other. Children's parties were in the village hall, and there was plenty of beautiful countryside that was perfect for nature walks, with fields of cows and sheep, tangled brambles and ivy-wrapped trees. It was the kind of place where getting stuck behind a tractor would be the usual reason for being late. Flowers and strawberries were sold on the side of the road, and there was plenty of work for the local thatchers. With very little else to do, it was all about making your own entertainment, which was perfect for the Middletons as they focused on arts and crafts, and outdoor sports. It was in their genes – Carole's father Ron was a talented painter, carpenter and baker, and had once made his wife Dorothy a violin at night school. Meanwhile, Michael's grandmother Olive painted watercolours and his grandfather Noel had a family orchestra, in which Michael's father played cello. Kate and Pippa learned to play the flute and sang in the choir. Kate, like her great-grandmother, enjoyed painting, and their grandmother Valerie taught the girls to sew. Valerie was also responsible for Kate's favourite fancy dress costume, which Kate explains was, 'A wonderful pair of clown dungarees … They were white with big red spots and she used a small hula hoop for the waistband – genius!'

The hub of the home was the kitchen. It was a long thin room with a sloping ceiling and not enough room for a table, but there was always something going on in there. Carole cooked and baked, and all of the children would help out. Carole, of course, loved marking an event, and so birthdays, public holidays and special occasions were all celebrated. And not just with an egg off the supermarket shelf for Easter, or a store-bought birthday cake. Although there was no snobbery about them and they thought there was nothing wrong with the simple pleasures – Kate's favourite party food was jelly – it was more to do with the whole family enjoying the ritual and camaraderie of creating things together. At Easter, they would make hard-boiled eggs marbled with food colouring, and Christmas was always a big deal. Kate, Pippa and James would spend December crafting their own cards and wreaths, making brandy butter and peppermint creams, and festooning their bedrooms with home-made paper chains. On Christmas Day, the TV was switched off and the family would go for long walks before opening their presents after supper.

The summer was a time to spend even more time outside – whether it was idyllic and golden, or a waterlogged disaster, there would be numerous outdoor activities. The Middletons had always been outdoorsy with a broad adventurous streak. When Kate's grandfather Peter retired, he and his wife sailed across the Atlantic to the Caribbean in a thirty-five-foot boat, and in 1976 the pair survived a shipwreck in the Bahamas. This spirit of adventure was inherited by their grandchildren, who loved throwing themselves into various outdoor pursuits including camping, sailing and hiking. Kate in particular was always a tomboy.

Since Michael was still working for BA, if they wanted to holiday overseas the whole family was eligible for standby tickets, which cost just ten per cent of the original price. The whole family would have had to dress smartly – no denim, men in suits and women in tights – and they wouldn't be able to check in their luggage because they wouldn't know if they would be definitely on the flight until the last minute, when they would carry their own luggage to the gate, and were the last ones to board.

In these years in Berkshire, now as a family of five with a growing business, the Middletons led a simple existence. Carole's parents Ron and Dorothy bought a house in nearby Pangbourne and Michael's parents Peter and Valerie lived over the border in Hampshire, so the children were surrounded by family growing up, and were close to their grandparents. In the summer, Peter would take his grandchildren sailing on the Hamble estuary near his home, where he would give them instructions and they would call out a jokey, 'Aye aye kipper!' He also made them a wooden pirate ship for them to play with in the garden.

There were annual holidays to the Lake District, where they would go walking, putting the picnic food together as a team effort before they set off. They would each have their one responsibility, whether it was making the sandwiches, gathering the snacks or stocking the rucksacks, and then they would load up with their provisions, which included Kendal mint cake and flapjacks, before heading out for the day. They would also camp out in their back garden, having midnight feasts and campfires, and Michael would rig up an Anglepoise lamp in the tent with an extension cord. They got on well with their neighbours and they enjoyed barbecues together. One played the banjo and they would sing campfire classics such as 'Ging Gang Goolie' and 'Row Your Boat'.

It sounds like the stuff of fiction, but this was Kate's childhood. Later on, this way of life must have been very attractive to the young William when he and Kate were first starting to get to know each other. Although his parents strived to create a warm and loving environment for their sons, and often succeeded, they were a couple at war and it would have shown. The Middleton upbringing was close, stable and simple, and while William's would have had some of those qualities some of the time, despite the best possible intentions the strained relations between Charles and Diana would have been impossible to hide.

Diana had wanted to instil a normality for her boys that involved trips to McDonald's and fairground rides at Disney World, but security, disguises and paparazzi meant it still wasn't the reality experienced by others. However many cheap burgers William ate, he still lived in palaces, and his life was inevitably threaded through with centuries of tradition, formality and protocol. Throughout his childhood there were staff everywhere, press outside and the weight of his destiny lying heavy on his shoulders. For Kate and her siblings, although they went to private school and had financial stability, their home lives were commonplace – they popped to the local shops and got involved with village life. While some have derided Kate for the simplicity and domesticity of her background, it has served her well, and it is sure to have been one of the things that was so appealing to William.

As the children got older, the celebrations became more ambitious – parties were themed, and imaginative cakes and treats were created. For one of James's birthday parties the theme was pirates, and there was a huge water-balloon fight in the garden, while Kate remembers her favourite party memory was a white rabbit marshmallow cake that Carole made for her seventh birthday.

The young Kate also made fledgling attempts in the kitchen, including a disastrous effort for one of James's birthdays: 'I tried making my brother's cake one year but I forgot to add the self-raising flour,' she later recalled on the Party Pieces website. 'Obviously, the cake never rose so I used the flat sponge and turned it into a trifle cake! We still managed to use candles and it's a great alternative for anyone who doesn't like cake. Not sure my brother agreed at the time!' James added, 'Boys don't like trifle when they should have had a pirate cake!'

It just goes to show the make-do-and-mend mentality in the Middletons' home that Kate didn't descend into gloom when her efforts went wrong, it was simply a matter of putting a positive spin on things. The Middleton way is not just a case of when life gives you lemons you make lemonade, but rather going that one step further, and using those lemons to make a beautifully presented and delicious lemon syllabub.

By the early nineties, the Middletons had registered the domain name Party Pieces online and the company was doing well. They had made a few additions to their home, adding in the garden a long shed with a high ceiling, power points and a phone line, which they used as an office, and building an extension to act as a playroom for the children, which was soon filled with books, toys, a TV and VHS player, with drawings from school on the walls.

Many uncomplimentary and vinegary comments have been made about Carole Middleton being a pushy, social-climbing mother, but they are rooted in jealousy and snobbery. After all, what mother doesn't want her children to have a better life than she had growing up? Aspiration is not a dirty word. Carole had started out with nothing, grew up in a small house in the middle of a council estate, and attended state schools. It was she who set up her own business from her own idea, and worked hard while raising three children. It was her husband who left his job to work full-time for her blossoming company, and years later she still works hard to keep the business running. She has raised her girls to be strong, fulfilled, healthy and thriving young women. Others have been called feminist role models for less. She even found the time to join in the parents' rounders match at school sports day. If Carole had trodden on people and treated them badly as she tried to make a better life for herself and her children, then perhaps there might be a reason for the sniping, but those who have known Carole unfailingly describe her as a friendly, warm and hard-working woman. Others have sniffed that Party Pieces was so successful because of the Middletons' association with the royal family, but the fact is the company did very well for fifteen years before Kate first met William.

It was only when Kate was eleven that she started boarding at St Andrew's, so for both Kate and Pippa their first time staying away from home on their own was with the Brownies. They had joined the First St Andrew's pack in Pangbourne in September 1990, when Kate was eight and Pippa had just turned seven, and the following Easter they went away to Brownie camp at

Macaroni Wood in the Cotswolds. They fed chickens, collected eggs, watched chicks hatch, bottle-fed lambs, rode horses and went for horse-and-cart rides. They also went to Cogges Manor Farm and an old-fashioned milking parlour for ice cream. Indoor activities included craft projects making puppets and Easter chicks, as well as helping out in the kitchen by peeling onions and potatoes. They also had to do housework around the place to earn their badges, before spending the night in sleeping bags on camp beds in dorms.

Meanwhile, Kate was thriving at school. She was popular and always surrounded by friends. She had looked after Pippa when she'd started two years after her, and the sisters have always been extremely close. Over her eight years at the school, Kate played hockey and tennis, was captain of the netball team, the highest scorer of the season in rounders, won the 200 metres, broke school records for swimming, high jump and long jump, and also enjoyed cross-country running. Additionally, she went on the annual skiing trips that were organized by the school. She also went on a school trip to Snowdonia, where they went gorge-walking and climbing over the rocky, wild landscape, which was second nature to her after her family trips to the Lake District.

'She was a 100-mph kind of girl and put full concentration into everything she did,' recalled her old 'house parent' Kevin Allford in an interview with the *Daily Mail*. 'She was a hard worker and would often take herself off to the classrooms to study when everyone else was playing.' Although later in life, when she entered the public eye, some expressed concern over Kate's slender frame, Kevin's wife Denise, her other 'house parent', explains that Kate has always been that slim. 'Catherine had a very high metabolic rate ... She had a tremendous appetite but because she put so much effort into everything she needed a constant supply of calories.'

Life for Kate wasn't just about the big outdoors, however. She was in the school's chamber orchestra and was later in the flute group the Tootie-Flooties with sister Pippa. She also sang in the choir, eventually becoming deputy head chorister. They performed locally outside pubs and restaurants for charity, and at St James's Church for the Christingle service on Christmas Eve, and then in 1994 when Kate was twelve, the choir entered the BBC's Song for Christmas competition and were one of fifty schools who received a commendation.

Although there were no pets in the Middleton home, there were a handful at the school including two guinea pigs called Pip and Squeak. Because her sister was called Pippa, it meant that Kate's nickname became Squeak. It was also at St Andrew's that she learned about Scottish customs. St Andrew's Day was celebrated, although haggis was substituted with meatloaf, but still served with neaps and tatties, and one pupil would read the Selkirk Grace. Pupils would later take part in the 'progressive games' that were unique to the school. They were played indoors and involved short five-minute games earning scores.

Discipline instilled by her parents had paid off and Kate made the most of her time and the various opportunities she had at St Andrew's. She loved the experience so much that when she left she told Carole she wanted to be a teacher when she was older. For a time, Kate also enjoyed treading the boards. While she was still at St Andrew's she would take part in public-speaking competitions, pantomimes and plays. She learned ballet and tap, and enjoyed drama workshops during her summer holidays. At odds with her reserved image is the fact that Kate often not only took part in many school productions, but usually played the lead role. In 1992, at the age of ten, she played Prince Charming in *Cinderella*, with plenty of thigh-slapping, and Eliza Doolittle in *My Fair Lady*, opposite Andrew Alexander who is now in the classical group Teatro. She also performed in *The Nutcracker*, and sang a solo in the summer concert. She was not only word perfect every time, but could sing well.

At the age of ten, she was not interested in boys, and was still more passionate about her sports and hobbies. She would watch when Prince William occasionally came to play hockey matches at the school, and couldn't have helped but wonder about what he was going through at the time. It was in 1992 that his parents officially separated, and due to the divorce of Princess Anne and Captain Mark Phillips, the separation of Prince Andrew and Sarah, Duchess of York, and the fire at Windsor Castle, the Queen would later refer to the year as her *annus horribilis*. After years of Charles and Diana's feuding spilling into the papers, criticism about which members of the family should receive money from the government, and disenchantment growing for a royal family that seemed out of touch with the modern world, their popularity was at an all-time low. At the time, William was keeping his head down at school and trying to take his mind off his families' problems. As well as Kate, most of the school would watch him play when his team visited, but it was another blond-haired William who was the next object of her affection.

CHAPTER THREE

'Yes, yes, dear William!'

Teetering on the edge of adolescence was a tall skinny girl with bobbed brown hair and braces. She was more concerned with sports socks and knee supports than eyeshadow and lip gloss. While other girls were beginning to experiment with makeup, fashion and boys, Kate stuck with what she knew and what made her comfortable. Her Uncle Gary said that she was always dressed for fun. Reassuringly for other awkward pre-teens, Kate had yet to grow into the polish and poise of her adult years. That wasn't her concern at the time. The boys in her class weren't interested in her yet and, for the most part, she wasn't interested in them either. As she celebrated her thirteenth birthday and entered what would be her last year at St Andrew's, she was still focused on her schoolwork, her sporting achievements and her passion for performing and the arts. She became a prefect and, before she left, she passed her flute and singing exams, and won the Calvert Cup for rounders and the Leslie Cup for outstanding overall sporting achievement for a girl.

She also trod the boards once more in a play called *Murder in the Red Barn*, which was based on a real-life murder in Suffolk in 1827 – and some of the dialogue proved to be strangely prophetic. Thirteen-year-old Kate played local woman Maria Marten, who was told by a fortune teller that she would meet 'a rich gentleman', to which Kate whispered theatrically to the audience, 'It is all I ever hoped for!' Asking, 'Will he fall in love with me? And marry me? Will he take me away from here?' She is told by the fortune teller, 'Yes! To London.' As she stood alone on the stage daydreaming about her future, she swooned, 'Rich and handsome … He'll fall in love with me … He'll marry me … London …' Later in the play a blond boy playing her beau, William, knelt before her and asked for her hand in marriage. Kate sighed theatrically and replied, 'Yes, yes, dear William!' In real life, William Corder then shot and killed Maria Marten and buried her in the red barn, but that, happily, is where the two tales divide. It was another sixteen years before Kate's real life blond-haired, floppy-fringed William fell in love with her and married her. As for London – she would not only move there, but was to become one of its most famous residents, with her face on postcards and her home a royal palace.

Even in 1995, the Middletons were already moving on in the world. The year Kate left St Andrews was also the year that Carole and Michael were able to buy a bigger property. Party Pieces had been doing so well that they were able to sell their first married home on Cock Lane for £158,000 and buy a new place in the nearby hamlet of Chapel Row for £250,000. The large detached country house with five bedrooms was called Oak Acre and was set in one-and-a-half acres of land. Kate chose a blue-and-cream colour scheme for her bedroom, while Pippa opted for red. Carole and Michael had some of the walls knocked through to create an open-plan feel, and later allowed the children to make use of the outhouse by having their friends over to listen to music. They also bought some old farm buildings in nearby Ashburton Common, which meant they had a place to store stock and could take on more staff.

Despite the move, it was very much business as usual for the whole family, as their nearest village of Bucklebury and the surrounding area was similar to where they had come from, just ten miles away. All around was green and leafy, with plenty of ancient oaks and fields – unless you wanted to pull your wellies on and go for a nice long walk, it was the kind of place where you would need to drive everywhere. The family always attended the August Bank Holiday fair and often frequented their local pub the Old Boot Inn. An eighteenth-century building with a contemporary interior, it wasn't the kind of gastro-pub that people would drive from miles around to visit, but was a comfortable and easy local with a log fire and a conservatory out the back. The Middletons made use of all the local amenities, and settled in easily; and in the autumn, Kate was bound for the prestigious Downe House School. The perky, high achiever was used to being among like-minded peers and had always been popular in a quiet, unassuming kind of way, so what came next was something of a shock.

Less than a ten-minute drive from home, Downe House in neighbouring Thatcham is made up of a large sprawl of complexes, including teaching and housing blocks, dotted around 110-acres of wooded parkland. Former pupils include Miranda Hart, Claire Balding and Sophie Dahl, and the school has a good reputation. As an indication of how well Party Pieces was doing in 1995, fees were £22,000 a year, and the Middletons had every intention of all three of their children being privately educated. Kate would have to acclimatize to suddenly being in an all-girls school, but she was close to her mother and her younger sister, and although she had always been a tomboy in her rough-and-tumble interests, she liked the company of girls. So how hard could it be?

She set about working hard, getting involved with the sporting teams and tentatively making new friends, but something about her rankled with some of the other girls, and they took a dislike to her. She was also set apart as different as she was one of only a few girls who didn't board and returned home after school. At a time in life when it is thought of as cool to be experimenting with drinking, smoking and boys, Kate was soft and sweet natured, and still more interested in her school work and sports. Former pupil Emma Sayle recalls, 'Downe House is a great school but it is a fighting school. She was bullied.' It was a huge shock for Kate.

Kate was the product of a loving, and safe childhood that was so idyllic it could have been lifted from the pages of an Enid Blyton book – with marshmallow cakes and rounds of 'Ging Gang Goolie' round the camp fire. Although she had travelled a little, she wasn't worldly-wise – she had romantic notions and old-fashioned values. Some of the girls there were from big cities and by the age of thirteen were precocious, sleek and somewhat jaded. Kate was therefore an easy target as a goodie-goodie for the harder more mature girls who were all about breaking the rules, challenging authority and establishing dominance.

They called her names, stole her books and when she sat down for lunch they would get up and move. Susan Cameron was headmistress when Kate was there and told the *Daily Mail*, 'Yes, there would be teasing … Girls are cliquey by nature and they can be rather cruel … They can sense those who are slightly weaker or who haven't shown their strengths yet, and it's those girls who are likely to end up being picked on or teased. I think it's fair to say [Kate] was unsettled and not particularly happy.'

After two terms, it became clear it just wasn't working, and was not likely to change, and so Carole and Michael took Kate out of Downe House, and enrolled her in the nearby and equally prestigious Marlborough College.

Everyone deals with bullying differently, and it can be hard to put a name to it when it is happening, but for others who are experiencing something similar, Kate is a good example of how someone can overcome bullying and blossom. She didn't flee at the first sign of trouble, she tried to make the best of her situation and stuck with something very difficult, but equally she knew when it was time to make a change. She later lent her support to those who have been through similar experiences when she and William selected the charity Beatbullying to be one of the organizations their wedding donations would benefit from. The official reason given for this was that Kate and William had chosen each charity because it had resonance with them and reflected issues in which they were both particularly interested.

Being fourteen isn't easy, starting a new school at that age also isn't easy, and starting two terms in, when everyone else has acclimatized and made friends, definitely isn't easy. Kate was not only facing the prospect of being the new girl again in the spring of 1996, but was still affected by the confidence-destroying incidents she had so recently left behind. But she was made of stern stuff. She picked herself up, dusted herself off and, dressed in her new uniform of white shirt with a dark-blue jumper and blue-and-green kilt, started at Marlborough College in Wiltshire at the beginning of the summer term.

Marlborough is, like St Andrew's school, very private and hidden behind large gates. Inside is a cluster of red-brick buildings, some clad in ivy, called 'Court' that are set around a perfectly manicured lawn. The main building is a Georgian mansion, which is used as one of the all-boys boarding houses, and around the lawn stand assorted other Georgian and Victorian buildings used as further boarding houses, the school's theatre and the English block. A Gothic chapel stands in one corner, containing Pre-Raphaelite paintings and stained glass by William Morris, who was a former pupil. The whole school was built beside the Marlborough Mound – a large grassy knoll thought to have been part of a Norman castle. Fanning out from the main court are trees, lawns and streams, six grass hockey pitches, ten netball courts and twenty-four tennis courts. At £27,000 a year, it was more expensive than Eton, and alumni include poet laureate Sir John Betjeman and actor James Mason. Prime Minister's wife Samantha Cameron was there before Kate and Princess Eugenie went there after Kate had left.

The college was divided into houses and each was home to around sixty to seventy pupils while Kate was there. Classes and sporting activities took place around or close to the central court, and main meals were eaten in the dining hall there. The houses were scattered around the grounds, a short walk away, and pupils would return to them for personal study, relaxation and sleep. They could pop back to their house at any time during the day, and each had a common room and small kitchen area where they could keep and make their own food. The houses were run by a house master or mistress, who acted as a parent figure, building a close relationship with each of the pupils in their care, mentoring them and overseeing their development. They managed the house sports, and were the main point of contact for a parent regarding their child. Additionally, they were supported by a 'dame' who would look after the domestic side of living arrangements such as washing and sewing, and who ran the cleaning staff. There was also a school counsellor called Mrs Bryant who visited twice a week. In the first year, the girls slept together in communal dormitories, moving on to shared 'bedsits' as they moved up through the school.

Kate was back in an environment with boys and girls mixed together, and this suited the young teenager. It was however decided that she would be placed in the all-girls residence of Elmhurst House, which had strong sporting links. It was a mid-nineteenth-century building with its own garden. Before she arrived, the dame Mrs Gould took the girls to one side and told them that a new girl was arriving and that she needed to be treated kindly because she hadn't been treated well at her previous school. Headmaster Ed Gold also came by the common room in Kate's first week to see how she was getting along. Things were going well and she was making friends with the girls in her dorm and settling in to her new surroundings.

The school day began when they were woken up by the bell at 7.30 and, after breakfast, classes started between 8.30 and 9 a.m., with lunch at 12.30, hockey practice at 1.30, and then more classes. There could be more hockey practice at 4.30 for half an hour, and then back to Elmhurst for a two-hour study period and supper. Meals could be eaten in the main hall, or the girls could make themselves something in their house kitchen

– Kate liked peanut butter, Dairylea triangles, hot pepperoni and Marmite. Her speciality was gooey microwaved Marmite sandwiches.

Following the blip at Downe House, life now continued as normal. She played hockey, tennis and netball, enjoyed cross-country running and worked hard, eventually becoming a prefect. Fellow pupil Kathryn Solari said she was, 'always really sweet and lovely. She was a very good girl and quite preppy – she always did the right thing – and she was very, very sporty.' While another, Charlie Leslie, recalls she was, 'Level-headed and down to earth ... an absolutely phenomenal girl – really popular, talented, creative and sporty.' Before long, Kate was not only getting stuck into the sports, but the extracurricular fun and games as well. She took part in a students' version of *Blind Date*, where she borrowed a lime-green blouse, black skirt and fishnets and wore a wig to dress up as Cilla Black and host the proceedings. She also took part in the 'house shout', which was like a glee club where she and three friends sang the *Friends* theme song 'I'll Be There For You'. It was an inclusive and warm environment and each girls' house was twinned with a boys' house – whichever was the closest in proximity. Elmhurst's 'brother' house was Barton, next door, and the two enjoyed friendly rivalry as well as camaraderie with many inter-house parties.

In the second year, Kate moved out of her dorm and shared a twin bedsit with her friend Jessica Hay. At the time, fourteen-year-old Prince William was starting to grace magazine covers. His parents had finally divorced that year and he had recently started at Eton, so he was very much in the public eye. *Time* magazine ran a full-page picture of him on their cover and, following the very public problems within the royal family that had fuelled the papers for most of the past decade, starkly asked, 'Can this boy save the monarchy?' While *People* magazine also ran William as a main image on their cover, proclaiming 'Look who's a teen idol!' He was becoming something of a pin-up along with the likes of *Romeo and Juliet*'s Leonardo DiCaprio and Ewan McGregor from *Trainspotting*. A poster of the young William had been left on the wall of Kate and Jessica's new living quarters by the previous inhabitants, but after a while the girls took it down. Kate customized their digs by putting up a picture of a Levi's model and of Kate Moss, who at the time was the fresh-faced ingénue girlfriend of Johnny Depp, and was the younger girl's style icon.

However, while Ms Moss favoured rock chic and vintage fashion, Kate the schoolgirl dressed in a low-key, simple way. Classmate Gemma Williamson told the *Daily Telegraph*, 'Kate never wore particularly fashionable or revealing clothes – just jeans and jumpers with discreet pearl earrings and lots of bangles.' The fifteen-year-old Kate was yet to find her fashion feet and at the time simply enjoyed messing around with her girlfriends and having innocent fun. Her pre-teen bob had been grown out and she wore her hair on her shoulders, dressing in blue jeans and vests and cardigans, accessorized with a tangle of little chains and necklaces. She was fresh-faced, natural and sporty, but hadn't yet started turning the boys' heads. The dormitories in all-boys Barton House would pin a list up on their door, naming girls who they liked at that time, but Kate was never on the list. She liked singing along to Whitney Houston, and at the time the Spice Girls were just bursting into the charts. The unassuming teen would have never believed that Posh Spice Victoria Beckham would later be at her wedding to Prince William – it would have been the stuff of schoolgirl fantasy.

In the summer of 1998, at the age of sixteen, Kate sat eleven GCSEs – all of which she passed. Afterwards, she and a big group of girls and boys celebrated in nearby Great Bedwyn – a quintessentially English spot surrounded by meadows and rivers. It was a favourite of the teenagers, and under a tree they would drink, chat, flirt and sunbathe. The boys would take wine and vodka and the girls would bring the food. After their exams, they all got drunk, apart from Kate. Her friend Jessica told the *News of the World* later, 'I never once saw her drunk. Even after our GCSEs finished, she only drank a few glugs of vodka.'

Kate did have a more rip-roaring night at a party hosted by her friend Alicia Fox-Pitt's brother, William, and left a lot less composed than when she arrived, but it was a rare occurrence. It seems she learned early that she didn't like the feeling of being drunk. It affected her quickly and she would be giggly and silly after a couple of drinks, and so while she was happy to play lookout for the girls who did want to sneak out and make mischief, she looked after herself and played by the rules.

Bo Bruce, the English singer-songwriter and contestant on the BBC TV show *The Voice* – whose full name is Lady Catherine Anna Brudenell-Bruce – was at school with Kate and Pippa, and recalls, 'They were such cool girls. We were on the hockey team and they were a laugh, successful and universally loved. There aren't any skeletons with those girls.'

That summer, Kate went overseas for the first time without her parents, travelling around Brazil and Argentina with the school hockey team. Not only did she triumph along with the rest of her teammates, losing just two games throughout the whole trip, but she also embraced the whole experience and grew up a little along the way. She kissed South American boys and drank in all of the new experiences, including a visit to the stunning Iguazu Falls. Bigger than Niagara, they are humid and tropical with pounding water and clouds of mist. In the words of her classmate Gemma, Kate came back from the summer holidays 'an absolute beauty'. Something had changed about her and she had blossomed, returning tanned and carefree. She had grown into her looks and, on the cusp of turning seventeen, she had filled out and was more poised and confident. She was, after all, a woman who had seen the world. She grew her hair longer and started to wear subtle makeup.

Boys at school started noticing her and she participated, along with other classmates, in the organized snog, where friends would act as intermediaries, passing a note to the object of the individuals' affection. The pair would then get together at the weekend, before going back to their respective dorms to compare notes. Kate's favourite was a tall boy with chiselled cheekbones and dirty-blond hair called Willem Marx. It was a fleeting teenage fancy, but the pair remained friends and socialized together in London on more than one occasion a decade later. It was well known that Kate was very picky with her affections and she didn't find many boys attractive – from an early age she had self-respect – and while she particularly liked Willem, she thought a lot of the other boys were 'rough'. She was very much a girl's girl and would go with friends every Wednesday to the Polly Tea Rooms for tea and blueberry muffins. By this time she wore the upper-school uniform of a long black skirt with shirt and jacket – the boys wore suits.

As her happy time at Marlborough was coming to an end, thoughts turned to what would come next. Kate had always been interested in art and decided to study history of art at university, but the there was the question of which one she would choose. At one point she was keen on Oxford Brookes, which was known for its history of art course, but she didn't have to decide just yet. Before that, there was a glorious summer in front of her and her gap year to take care of. She finally left Marlborough with three A levels in chemistry, biology and art. She had done herself proud – they were above-average results and meant that she would have her pick of the best universities in the country.

CHAPTER FOUR

First-aid and porridge
in Patagonia

The gap year has become as much a part of a middle-class education as completing A levels and going to a good university. Sandwiched between the two, it is a chance to work overseas, see the world and experience a bit of life before starting higher education. While some teens experiment with roadside food stands, hair-wraps and mind-altering substances, Kate headed to Florence in Tuscany for culture and education. There she studied Italian at the British Institute for three months. She lived in a flat with a little stone staircase above a deli, with three other girls including Chris Rea's niece Alice Whitaker. Kate embraced the history and romance of the medieval city. Known as the birthplace of the Renaissance, Florence is laced with bustling squares, ancient palaces and galleries, while church bells ring out throughout the day. It is a city so rich in culture that many visitors have suffered from Stendhal syndrome – dizziness, fainting and hallucinations after being faced with the overwhelming abundance of art. It was the perfect setting for the girl who would soon be starting a history of art degree.

She explored the city with her camera, walking the cobbled streets that have been trodden for a millennia, soaking up the surroundings and taking pictures of one incredible sight after another. There were plenty to chose from – from the Vecchio Bridge over the River Arno overhanging with old jewellery shops, to the famous Duomo of Florence Cathedral and the riches-filled church of Santa Croce. In the warmth of a Florentine autumn, languid afternoons melted into evening and the girls embraced the pavement-café culture. They would head to the L'Art Bar in Via del Moro for happy-hour cocktails and hang out with other school-leavers. The local boys buzzed around her, but she wasn't interested in them. She had been seeing a fellow Marlborough student called Harry, who was also studying in Florence on a different course, although it wasn't to last as he didn't want to 'commit'. Her parents came to visit halfway through her course, and she showed them the sights. They stayed in a local hotel and took her and her friends out for drinks in the evening. As December approached, the course finished and Kate headed back home to Berkshire for Christmas with her family, but shortly after celebrating her nineteenth birthday she was packing again. Instead of the sun-honeyed cobbles and ancient squares of Florence, she was bundling up in waterproofs and thermals and heading to Chile.

It wasn't her first time in South America, as she had toured with the school's hockey team through Argentina and Brazil in the summer when she was sixteen. This time she was learning and working, along with 150 other young people as part of a group organized by Operation Raleigh. 'One of Raleigh's key purposes is personal development,' explains Malcolm Sutherland, who was Kate's expedition leader. 'You are put into an environment which is probably out of your comfort zone in a fairly diverse group of people, and you have to make it work.' Of the 150 young people out there, some were privately educated like Kate, but others were young offenders or had come out of drugs rehabilitation programmes, so she would be with a very mixed group of people.

Prince William had been part of a team who had been to the same part of Chile three months earlier, and many of the workers out there experienced spending time with both him and Kate. It has been suggested that Kate followed William to Chile and St Andrews in an attempt to ingratiate herself with him, but she had been to an Operation Raleigh selection weekend the previous summer, where potential volunteers were told about the different trips on offer, and had already made her decision to go to Chile before it was announced that was where William was going. (Additionally, William's press team didn't announce which university he was going to until the following autumn, by which time Kate had already made her choice of St Andrews. So the fact that Kate and William both went to Chile with Operation Raleigh, and then to the University of St Andrews meant nothing more than they had similar interests.)

Before she left for Chile, Kate attended a briefing day with the others and was taught about Chilean culture, local government and the projects she would be working on, plus there were ice-breaking tasks so that people could get to know each other a little more. They were told to bring waterproofs, warm clothes, a sleeping bag and a sleeping mat, and that the three months' worth of gear that they brought would need to fit into one rucksack. They were to be there at the tail end of the Chilean summer heading into winter, and the weather was quite British – changeable with a bit of sun, but a lot of cold weather and a lot of rain. At the end of January, Kate met the other 150 volunteers at the airport and they flew to Chile together. For the first five days, they acclimatized to the altitude and embarked on a training package that involved learning more about the country as well as first aid, how to operate radio systems and how to cook for large groups of people. They were then divided into groups of twelve along with two members of staff.

Kate and her team then set out for three weeks of trekking in Patagonia, where she and the rest of the group tackled river crossings, climbed peaks and pitched their tents at night, learning about their surroundings and survival techniques from the group leaders as they went along. They all slept in two-person tents and, as well as carrying their own rucksacks, would split the camping equipment and cooking supplies to carry between them. As they were constantly on the move in a remote area, the food was basic and easy to prepare, with no meat or dairy and very little fresh food. It was porridge for breakfast and a lot of rice, pasta and dehydrated packet food in the evenings, when all they needed to do was to add hot water. They cooked and ate as a group, and there was a no alcohol policy, so there were lots of early nights after an exhausting day of exploring.

Each day, they would take turns to be in charge of different responsibilities, so one day Kate was the team leader, another she was in charge of the cooking and another she was in charge of communications back to the field base. 'She was a quietly strong person,' Malcolm Sutherland recalls. 'She wasn't extrovert, she wasn't trying to be anything, she was just strong and she got on with it without any fussing. She was a good team-member and good at working with other people rather than being the one who would jump up and try to take over.'

At the end of the three weeks, everyone was mixed up into totally new groups, before heading off to the next three weeks of the expedition, which was to be spent on a marine survey. Kate piled into the bus with the others for the seven-hour journey to Tortel, before taking a boat out to a small archipelago. This time they carried rigid inflatable boats and went out for days at a time to cover as much of the shoreline as possible, camping on beaches and working with scientists conducting marine animal surveys. Kate helped collect data on different organisms and sea life for the environmental project.

For the final leg of the trip, Kate headed back to the mainland to spend three weeks working on a community project, which for her meant helping to build a fire station. It was another remote area, with just around 200 people living nearby, one school and one shop. This time she stayed in a big communal building with all the other volunteers, sleeping in one huge room in their sleeping bags. They were given an allowance to spend on fresh food and would buy meat from the local farmer. In the evenings they would play cards and other games. Kate particularly responded to a short trip she made. 'We had a relationship with the local school,' Malcolm Sutherland recalls. 'We would encourage the volunteers to go down there with one of our staff as translator, so they could meet the kids and the teachers, and I know that Kate absolutely loved that. It's not everyone's cup of tea, but I remember she loved interacting with the local people and the children.'

Rachel Humphrey, who was one of the group leaders on the

trip, said, 'Kate had a certain presence. She was a very attractive girl, she was a very popular girl. Particularly popular with the boys, and she was a great member of the expedition. But she was always very in control of herself and impeccably behaved.'

After roughing it in Chile, Kate was home again in time for summer, and spent the last part of her gap year working in the slightly more genteel surroundings of corporate regattas off the South Coast of England. She had secured herself a job as a crew member on the BT Global Challenge on the Solent. It was physical work, and meant working long days as she looked after guests. Her day would start early, as she scrubbed the yacht she was assigned to, then loaded the food and drinks on board and served coffee and breakfast to the arriving guests. She would then go through the safety procedures with them and helped them hoist the sails, making them feel involved with the sailing process while topping up their drinks. One of the job requirements was that the crew had to have good social skills, and throughout the remainder of the day, Kate would then mingle with the guests, making them feel comfortable, and mastering the art of charming chitchat. This talent was to prove useful later in her royal life, when mixing with crowds during public walkabouts and attending official events with people she has only just met, building instant rapport and conveying approachability.

At the end of each day on the yachts, she would help get the sails down and clean the boat. It was a long day and the young crew were on their feet for all of it, they had to be 'on' and also be useful. But it was worth it – Kate liked the way of life and liked being on the water all day. In the evenings, the workers would often pile into Los Marinos tapas bar, and at the end of the night tumble into their cabins onboard the boat. She became friends with a local boy, Ian Henry, who worked on another boat, and when the Middletons took their family away to Barbados in August before Kate went off to university, Ian went too.

As the summer tans began to fade, Kate made the long journey from Berkshire to St Andrews on the west coast of Scotland. She was leaving Ian behind and starting a new life. The small medieval town is situated in Fife, fifty miles north of Edinburgh. It is full of grey sandstone buildings, which from around the wind-whipped coast look like they have been enchanted so that they huddle together for warmth. During term time, students make up one third of the population. Out of term, they evaporate back to family homes. The beach, West Sands, which was made famous by the race scene in *Chariots of Fire*, runs alongside it – vast and seemingly endless, it is mirrored with a huge expanse of sky, and has a bitter cold wind slicing in off the North Sea. The university is regarded as one of the best in the country, and had previously been attended by writer Fay Weldon and Olympic cyclist Sir Chris Hoy. It was also Scotland's first university, and the third oldest in the English-speaking world, being founded in 1413, and has come to be known for its School of Art History. Application for all courses rose there by forty-four per cent when it was announced that Prince William was to go to there, but by that time Kate had already accepted her offer.

Kate started university on 23 September 2001, along with most of the other new students, but a certain prince was nowhere to be seen for the first few weeks. It had been decided it was best if William skipped Freshers' Week – traditionally a time when new students fall in and out of love, bars and beds. There was also an agreement struck between the press and his father's office at Clarence House that the prince would be allowed to go through his education without being followed or harassed, and in exchange he would conduct interviews and pose for photos at key points. But for now, in the initial few weeks, he sensibly stayed away. It must have been tough for him knowing that everyone else was cracking on with their university life and getting to know each other, and that by the time he arrived alliances would already have been formed and the new environment become accustomed to. Of course, following her experience leaving Downe House and starting late at Marlborough, Kate would have known how he was feeling.

When Kate arrived, she set about making herself at home. She had been lucky enough to get a room in St Salvator's halls of residence, which were widely regarded as the best. Right in the centre of town but tucked back off the road, and conveniently close to the history of art block – these halls were to be her home for the next year, and her parents had paid £2,000 for a year's rent. The building was grand and built from grey sandstone, with a large grassy space out the front full of trees and flowerbeds. Inside, the hallway had high ceilings and was full of light, with a winding staircase leading to the first, second and third floors of bedrooms, which had shared bathroom and kitchen facilities. To the right of the entrance was the oak-panelled common room, which looked something like a gentlemen's club – with floor-to-ceiling windows, a grand piano, a fireplace and upholstered armchairs around tables. Racks of newspapers, and pictures of past students lined the walls. The dining hall on the other side was decorated with heavy oil paintings from the Scottish Enlightenment and stained glass windows, while the computer room contained the students' pigeonholes for their post, which they would need their room key to access. Also on the ground floor were the laundry, and a games room with snooker table, dartboard and table tennis. Each halls of residence was looked after by a warden, who was also the student's main point of contact about anything relating to their living arrangements while they were there. There was also a porter who looked after security, and cleaners whom the students knew by name and would often chat to.

Some halls were known for having smaller rooms, or bunk beds, or the buildings weren't as attractive, but St Salvator's – or 'Sallies' as it was known – had it all, plus many of the rooms overlooked the North Sea. All the rooms had character, they were different shapes and sizes, and they were furnished in the same way – painted cream, with burgundy-flecked carpet. Kate was in a shared room, with a pair of single beds, a mahogany-coloured double wardrobe with full-length mirror, wash basin, book shelf and two desks. Being in close proximity with a complete stranger is very intimate, and it was another situation where it was to Kate's advantage that she was self-assured, friendly and well mannered. It helped that her roommate, Sara Bates, was a quiet and sweet girl. Their room was on the first floor of the four-floor building and the girls kept it neat and organized. There was a big noticeboard on the wall above Kate's desk and over the coming weeks and months she would fill it with photos of her friends.

Kate threw herself into Freshers' Week, the events of which were not only attended by the newcomers, but are so fun and well organized that students from all other years go as well. It's a pivotal time for the new students because of a one particular St Andrews tradition. After the social whirl is over, freshers will decide who they want to be their 'parents' while they are initially finding their way at the university, and they usually select a 'mum' and a 'dad' around this time. Over their years they will accumulate 'brothers', 'sisters', 'aunts', 'uncles' and even 'grandparents'. Then at Raisin Weekend in November, a few days of partying culminates in the student visiting their 'dad' on a Sunday night for drinks, and their 'mum' on the Monday morning who will dress them in a comical way for the foam fight in the main quad, next to Sallies. The tradition started when 'parents' would give the 'children' a receipt stating they would look after them, and the 'children' would say thank you with a gift of raisins. Over time, the receipt has turned into more comedic items such as fried eggs or jelly – which are difficult to keep hold of in a foam fight – and the raisins have been replaced with a bottle of wine. When Kate visited her 'mum' on the Monday morning, she was dressed in pigtails, bib and loo roll, with red lipstick on her cheeks before being covered in foam by her fellow freshers. William missed Freshers' Week and later also missed Raisin Weekend.

Shortly before his arrival, it was explained to the Sallies' residents by their hall warden that William would be joining them. It meant that not only was Kate going to be on the same course as the prince but they would also be living in the same building. Shortly afterwards, William arrived with his father the Prince of Wales, with just the minimum of fuss, and he moved into his room on the second floor. He didn't share with anyone and his room had a specially reinforced en-suite bathroom that could be used as a bunker if there were signs of danger, but apart from that he was just another student … ish.

William Arthur Philip Louis Windsor was born on the 21 June 1982. His parents, the Prince and Princess of Wales, had been married for a year. When he was born, the royal family were riding high in the eyes of the public. The Queen was loved and respected, the Silver Jubilee a few years earlier had seen people lining the streets, snapping up paraphernalia and hosting street parties. Hot on the heels of the jubilee was the whirlwind romance of Prince Charles and his nineteen-year-old sweetheart Lady Diana Spencer. With one sweep of her eyelashes the country was hooked, and they couldn't get enough of the blushing princess-to-be. Charles and Diana were dating for just six months and engaged for just five before they got married, and by the time they returned from their honeymoon in Balmoral, Diana was pregnant with William. It meant that for Charles and Diana, the timescale from their first date to the birth of their first child spanned only twenty-three months, and Diana was still just twenty-one years old.

Two years later, William was joined by younger brother Harry, but by that point the relationship between his parents was damaged beyond repair. Charles and Diana's expectations for the marriage were not mutually compatible. Charles was from the old school of the royal family, putting duty before his emotions, and still had feelings for his ex-girlfriend Camilla Parker Bowles. Diana was emotional, inexperienced and given no training in how to cope with life in the royal court. As is the way in the royal family, Charles had been taught to lead with his head. Diana led with her heart. This wasn't to say that Charles was wrong – they were just very different people who were simply not well suited. Throughout William's childhood, both parents strived to make it as happy and fulfilled as possible, and while his parents were leading increasingly separate lives, he had a strong relationship with both, as well as his brother, Harry..

William grew into a shy adolescent, and tried to shield

himself from the photographers behind his long fringe. In himself he knew his mind, but he wasn't entirely comfortable in public. He grew up seeing Diana hounded by the paparazzi, experiencing them clustering around her, preventing her from driving safely and upsetting her. Occasionally, things would get physical and protection officers and photographers would clash. When Diana died in a car accident when he was just fifteen, not only did he lose his beloved mother, who was also like a friend to him, but it also instilled in him a deep loathing of the paparazzi.

In order to be able to study properly, the deal had been struck so that he would be left alone by the press to study in peace. On his arrival at the University of St Andrew's, William was tall, athletic, tanned and blond, and wore jeans and a navy jumper with a light-blue shirt underneath.

Kate, meanwhile, was tall, athletic, tanned and brunette. Lots of boys were already interested in her, and by the end of Freshers' Week, she was known as the prettiest girl in Sallies. New friend Laura Warshauer – who is now a recording artist known as Gigi Rowe – lived down the hall from William and studied History of Art with them both. She remembers the first time she met Kate. 'She was sitting in the common room and she had a blue sweater over a white shirt,' Laura recalls. 'Her hair was long and curly and she was sitting upright. Before I even met her I was struck by her presence. She has that wow factor.' It seems that later on, when Kate was preparing for life in a public role, she didn't need a lot of training, since, Laura adds, 'She radiates this warmth. She has that way of putting people at ease and making them feel comfortable.'

The campus was small, and since Kate and William were on the same course and living in the same building, it wasn't long before they met for the first time. Later, in their engagement interview with Tom Bradby, Kate recalled, 'I went bright red and sort of scuttled off feeling very shy,' while William revealed, 'When I first met Kate I knew there was something very special about her. I knew there was something I wanted to explore there, but we ended up becoming friends for a while.'

The pair kept bumping into one another and it was obvious they took a shine to each other from very early on. They joked and bantered, and bonded over things they found they had in common. While watching a rugby match together on the sidelines, it became apparent to William that Kate knew what she was talking about and genuinely enjoyed the sport. They also talked about their gap years as they had both been to Chile and had both worked on marine monitoring projects – Kate while she was in Chile and William on another part of his gap year on the island of Rodrigues in the Indian Ocean. They had also both done some sailing – Kate in the Solent that summer, and William when he was younger in Africa.

'They had fun natural banter very early on,' recalls Laura. 'They would tease each other. It was a twinkle in the eye – the delivery of what was said.'

As well as the obvious chemistry, they also supported each other from the earliest days of their friendship. They went to get fish and chips one night and Kate forgot her wallet so William went back and got it for her, then in the lecture hall it was hot and Laura recalls, 'Kate came in with two waters – one for her and one for Will.'

Although things were bubbling under nicely, they were just nineteen years old, with minds and hormones in a whirl. William had been in a relationship with Arabella Musgrave before he moved to St Andrews. They had known each other for years, but had got together over the summer at a house party and had spent as much time together as possible before he went away. They had decided it was for the best if they split before he started university, but he was still thinking about her. He had also started seeing fellow student Carly Massy-Birch, who was in her second year, and with whom he slipped into an easy relationship – going to dinner parties with friends and enjoying Sunday mornings with the papers.

Meanwhile, Kate had met a fourth-year student, Rupert Finch, at one of the freshers' balls, and they had started seeing each other. He was tall, dark, handsome, sporty, wealthy and was considered a complete catch by the other students. 'Kate and Rupert were a bit of a golden couple,' recalls their university friend Michael Choong. 'Everyone wanted to go out with Kate, and Rupert was a real character and had lots of admirers. People saw them as two of the most eligible people in town. She didn't date anyone else.'

Rupert and his housemates would throw champagne-fuelled parties, and although Kate and Rupert's relationship wasn't as established as William and Carly's, both Kate and William certainly both had enough to be occupying them at the time.

There was also the matter of settling into the routine of studying. Most of their lectures and tutorials were held a short walk away, while their tutors were based in the art history block, just across the road.

The town was the perfect backdrop for young students living on their own for the first time – it was so small they could walk everywhere and it had a safe atmosphere where everyone knew each other. From their halls they could hear the roar of the sea at night and seagulls during the day. They would sometimes walk on the beach with its grassy sand dunes and wooden fences bleached out by the elements. At night, they would hang out at the Westport Bar, which was relaxed and contemporary, with wooden floorboards, cheap tasty food and a good-sized dance floor. No one would make the effort to dress up, and nights were always casual. On Fridays, they would go to Bop, the weekly club night at the Student Union.

During their first year, both Kate and William attended a 'high table' in their halls, where a small group of students are selected for a formal dinner with a prominent member of the community, and university staff. They dressed formally in the scarlet undergraduate gowns and Latin grace was said by the warden. Their halls provided breakfast, lunch and dinner every day, but at weekends the students fended for themselves and would wander into town for dinner, order a takeaway or cook together. There were several nights in Sallies where they would gather round for plates of home-cooked lasagne and drink red wine out of disposable plastic glasses bought from Woolworths.

Despite the cosy friendship and camaraderie between William and Kate, there were two instances that got tongues wagging that there might be something more between them. In October, there was a house party on nearby Hope Street, and one of the female partygoers was overtly flirting with William. He chatted to her for a while but it was getting awkward, and Kate walked across the room and put both her arms around him, so he was able to say to the girl, 'Sorry, I have a girlfriend,' before mouthing to Kate, 'Thank you.'

Laura Warshauer witnessed the gesture and recalls, 'This was in October. School started in September! I remember thinking no one else could have pulled that off. It was so natural. They had each other's backs.' Laura was also there the following month at an extravagant Harry Potter-themed birthday party.

It was held in Wemyss Castle nearby and everyone had to wear a costume and bring a bottle and a sleeping bag. There was a charity auction and William paid £200 for a date with Kate, and they later danced together. The next day, Laura says that William had Kate's back once again: 'We had a break for reading week. I was going to meet my sister in Paris and Kate was going home, so we were meant to be sharing a cab to the airport together, but then Will offered Kate a lift to the airport, so I got in on that ride.'

William had grown up being very aware of the fact that people would want to get to know him for who he is, and had developed a keen sense for those whose intentions were superficial. Around this time, there were girls throwing themselves at him, waiting for him outside rooms and stumbling up to him on nights out. Kate stuck out for him because she was composed and confident but not the centre of attention, just quietly self-assured. Plus, they genuinely had things in common and shared a similar sense of humour. He later said, 'We spent a lot of time with each other, had a giggle, had lots of fun, realized we shared the same interests and had a really good time. She's got a naughty sense of humour, which helps me because I've got a naughty sense of humour.'

He would always eat breakfast with a small group of friends and it wasn't long before Kate was one of them. The pair would also sometimes go for a run or a swim together in the Old Course Hotel. William drew his friends close, including his fellow Old Etonians Fergus Boyd and Alasdair Coutts-Wood, and new friends Oli Baker, Olli Chadwick-Healey, Graham Booth and Charlie Nelson. Collectively, they were known as 'Sallies' boys'. Kate slipped straight in with them, and when there was a birthday celebration for Laura in December, the card was signed 'from Will, Charlie, Oli and last but not least, Kate'. She had also struck up close friendships with Lady Virginia 'Ginny' Fraser, whom she knew from Downe House, and Olivia Bleasdale and Bryony Daniels, who were other female friends of William's.

As the nights drew in and the days got shorter and darker, William had what he later described as a 'wobble'. He was safe and protected by a close circle of friends at St Andrews, but he was also isolated. He was used to the space and freedom of his father's country home of Highgrove in Gloucestershire, and the bright lights and razzle-dazzle of London. Unlike in English universities, where courses usually last three years, in Scottish universities they last for four. It was a daunting prospect. He felt like he was doing the wrong course, and he would escape at weekends a lot, going to see family at Balmoral, visiting friends at other universities, and travelling back down south to see family. After splitting with Carly, he would also meet with his ex, Arabella. Kate was comfortable, happy and consistent in St Andrews, but her new close friend was not so sure.

CHAPTER FIVE

Falling in love

O ver the Christmas break, Kate and William stayed in touch. He wasn't happy, but it wouldn't look good if he dropped out of university after just one term, and even if he did, what then? He spoke to his family and the university about his options, and he also spoke to the girl who he was already leaning on and whose opinion he respected. Kate offered her support, helping him decide it might be a better option to stay where he was, but to change courses at the end of the first year. When they returned to St Andrews in January, the two friends picked up where they had left off. They were both active and outdoorsy – Kate played hockey, and William went surfing and played rugby, while they also went swimming and played tennis together. They also had a thriving social life, and when it came to the annual student fashion show – a way to mix fun with raising money for charity – Kate was up for participating.

The dress was meant to be worn as a calf-length skirt. It was a vapour of an item – a gauzy slip trimmed with blue ribbon, which, when worn as a dress, fell to mid-thigh. Kate hadn't done any acting since she was at school but the sweet-natured girl followed in the footsteps of her teenage icon, Kate Moss, and drew on her poise to strut her stuff at the charity fashion show, which was held in the Students' Union. Just when people thought they knew her, here she was appearing in public in a see-through dress with black underwear, a thousand-yard stare and an ice-cold high-fashion pout. If Kate and William were in a film, this was the moment when the heroine appears at the top of the staircase in a ball gown and glides slowly down as the hero sees her with new eyes. In this case, William had paid £200 for a front-row seat, and whispered to his friend, 'Wow, Kate's hot!'

Michael Choong recalls, 'I did not expect Kate to wear anything like that – it was not in keeping with her character at all.' The show was one of the events of the year – champagne-fuelled with banging house music. 'There was nothing amateur about it,' Michael says. 'It was a very professionally put-together thing, with sponsors and an amazing light show.'

With her hair twizzled in ribbons, Kate also sashayed down in a skin-tight black outfit, a gaudy fuzzy jumper and again half-naked with their friend Fergus. While he was stripped to the waist in just his trousers, Kate wore a white strapless bra with a black skirt pulled down on the hip to show off the matching white knickers. There was a house party afterwards, and as everyone drank and danced the night away, a giddy William leaned in to kiss Kate. Aware they were in a room full of people, she backed away. It wasn't the right time yet.

Their friendship continued to strengthen and they decided

that at the beginning of their second year they would move in together, along with their close friends Fergus and Olivia. By that time, Kate had split from Rupert, which meant that she and William were now both single. Celebrating the end of exams was a messier affair than normal and Kate broke with her usual composure. The halls held an unofficial fun awards ceremony at the end of the year with lots of light-hearted categories – Oli and Fergus won 'best couple' because they were never apart, while Kate won prettiest girl in the dorm. It had been an incredible year for her. She had gone from being the blushing girl who scuttled away from a prince to an underwear-clad catwalk queen. She had made new friends and carved out a home for herself in a blustery corner of Scotland. And she still had another three years to go. That summer, the prettiest girl in Sallies worked at the Henley Regatta, where she served champagne from the Snatch bar and was paid £5.25 an hour.

In September 2002, when everyone reassembled in St Andrews, Kate, William, Fergus and Olivia moved into 13a Hope Street, just around the corner from their first-year halls. After a year of friendship, Kate was used to William's protection officers, who, though always close to him, kept a discreet distance. However, this was the first time she encountered certain things that had been a fact of William's life since birth, and were increasingly to become her future. Their new home was fitted with bulletproof windows, a bomb-proof front door, and a state-of-the-art laser security system, while his protection officers lived nearby. For £100 a week each, the four housemates rented the two top floors and shared the cleaning.

Hope Street itself is made of up two neat rows of Georgian townhouses and was full of other student properties. The flats were all similar and not the most luxurious inside, but Hope Street was the most sought-after area for students. Inside 13a there were huge bedrooms with large windows that let in a lot of light, a little galley kitchen, open-plan living-and-dining room, and it had its own private garden. William took the bins out and left a tip for the binmen at Christmas, but only Kate was organized enough to register on the electoral roll while they lived there. They tried to install a cleaning rota but that soon descended into chaos.

Following his 'wobble' during the first year and his decision to switch from art history to geography, William was much happier and enjoying his studies.

Along with their other friends, the housemates enjoyed nights out all over town. Some of their local favourite spots included Ma Bells bar in the basement of the Golf Hotel. It was not solely a student hangout, upstairs was more elegant and traditional, with a cocktail bar and tartan carpets, and this was where they served salmon teriyaki, which Kate claimed was the best cure for a hangover. Downstairs was for students, and it was more relaxed, with wooden floorboards, big battered leather sofas and a basic range of drinks. Kate, along with the rest of her friends, would have a few glasses from their jugs of house cocktail. The Gin House (now called The Rule) was dimly lit and cavernous, and great for piling into en masse. It was cheap and cheerful, with wooden floorboards and a mezzanine balcony. The friends would also frequent the artfully mismatched fine-cuisine restaurant the Dolls' House, which was owned by TV presenter Carol Smillie. This too was not just a student haunt – although there were plenty of 'happy hours' and raucous student nights, Kate, William and their friends equally liked the more sophisticated places as well. They would also attend parties at other people's flats – however, if William was going, the host would receive a call from his protection team and they would do a security check before he arrived. Kate favoured gin and tonic or a glass of wine on their nights out, while William's tipple was Jack Daniel's and Coke or a pint of cider.

Kate and William would also spend a lot of time together at home. There were quiet nights in listening to music and cooking – house favourites included curries and pasta – or watching DVDs with a takeaway from curry house Balaka, or fish and chips from the Anstruther Fish Bar.

The growing bond went deeper than just DVDs on the sofa. It had recently been a difficult time for William and his family. Princess Margaret had died in February 2002, and although he was lucky to be surrounded by many close family members, she was the Queen's only sister and her death affected them all, as Margaret had also been William's neighbour as he was growing up in Kensington Palace. His great-grandmother the Queen Mother died less than two months later. The last time William had seen her was at Princess Margaret's funeral and it was a double blow that cast a dark shadow over the Queen's Golden Jubilee year.

Additionally, two months after Kate and William moved in together, William also had to endure the effects of the Paul Burrell trial, which was all over the papers. Diana's former butler had been accused of stealing several million pounds worth of items from her estate, and her family, the Spencers, were prosecuting him. Burrell had previously been a footman to the Queen, and following Diana's death he had requested a meeting with the her, at which he told her that he was taking a few papers for safekeeping. Around the time of the trial, the Queen mentioned this to Prince Charles, who told his private secretary and the trial dramatically collapsed on 1 November. It was yet another saga which, for William, attached further painful associations to the loss of his mother.

And then in December, William's best friend Thomas van Straubenzee lost his eighteen-year-old younger brother Henry in a car crash. Real life had penetrated William's student bubble and Kate was there for him throughout it all. Kate had been fortunate to have a tight-knit family around her growing up, and was a reassuring and stabilizing presence for the prince in this time of personal turbulence. This is how the seeds of their relationship were sown – light years away from the ceremony and duty associated with a royal coupling, a million miles from the pomp and the tradition. This was a boy and a girl hidden away in a little student house that looked the same as its neighbours, in a remote corner of Scotland, who were slowly feeling their way to see if a special friendship could be something more.

In November 2002, William took a group of sixteen friends shooting on his grandmother's Sandringham estate. The friends stayed in Wood Farm, which is a smaller property separate from the impressive main house and, although it still had a sizeable five bedrooms, questions were raised in the press about what the sleeping arrangements were – some of the party would certainly be sharing rooms, but in what capacity? It was the first time Kate and William were photographed together, but because the picture was taken on private property it couldn't be used in British publications. William was photographed with different female friends all the time, and there was no indication that he and Kate were anything more than friends.

As well as hanging out with the Sallies boys, Kate also had her own girlfriends, including Bryony Gordon, Ginny Fraser, Leonora Gummer and Sandrine Janet, a French student who was dating Kate's flatmate Fergus. Her sister Pippa would come up to visit and accompany Kate to balls organized by the golf or rugby clubs. Kate would also spend her time watching the rugby with her girlfriends, and Michael Choong remembers how unfussy she was: 'There was this one time she was watching and she was feeling cold, and one of the guys offered her his rugby waterproof. She had no qualms about wearing this sweaty boy's rugby kit. I thought it was cute. Will was there in his grubby hood and that would sum them up at that time – they were just typical students.'

They were first photographed together publicly at a rugby match they were both watching in May 2003, and it prompted speculation that there was something going on between them. When Kate's father Michael was approached by the press, he told them, 'I can categorically confirm they are no more than good friends. There are two boys and two girls sharing a flat at university. They are together all the time because they are the best of pals, and yes, cameramen are going to get photos of them together. But there is nothing more to it than that. We are very much amused at the thought of being in-laws to Prince William, but I don't think it's going to happen.'

Kate and William were slowly becoming involved, but the simple truth was that they had not yet worked out exactly what they wanted to happen between the two of them. Many university friendships cautiously edge into unknown territory, and sometimes there is simply no definition as to what they are to each other in other people's terms. Because of William's royal status, if they were to become a proper couple, Kate would be making a big step, and both of them wanted to make sure of what they had before sharing it with anyone else.

As the relationship began to grow inside the cocoon of

13a Hope Street, to the outside world things still looked the same. The pair left the house at different times, and were not demonstrative in public. Because of the arrangement that had been made with the press when William first started at St Andrews, there weren't photographers hanging out of trees or pursuing him, so the relationship had time and space to develop with no outside pressures. In his engagement interview with Tom Bradby William said, 'We moved in together as friends ... and it blossomed from there. We saw more of each other, hung out a bit more and stuff happened.'

In the early stages of their romance, they didn't socialize much together outside of the house as a couple. William would sometimes try to impress Kate by cooking her something fancy, but would ruin it, and she would have to come and salvage the remains. So when it came to hosting dinner parties, the duties were split. The boys would go and buy the food and the girls would make dinner. William would always produce a bottle of Jack Daniel's, and they would play drinking games, including 'I've never ...' where the person whose turn it was completed the sentence with something they had never done, and the people in the room who had done it had to take a drink. In Katie Nicholl's biography *William and Harry*, she recounts that on one occasion William's first-year ex, Carly, came for dinner and said, 'I've never dated two people in this room.' As William fumed and took a drink, Kate was unimpressed.

Living together and having housemates like a ring of steel around them helped them work out exactly what they were slowly, in a relaxed way. In that manner, in the summer of 2003, they both attended each other's twenty-first birthday party. Although Kate had turned twenty-one in January, she held off the big celebrations until a better time, as she had only just returned to St Andrews after the Christmas break and wanted to celebrate at her parents' house. Kate and William both loved fancy dress. Kate had, of course, grown up with a keen sense of occasion, and was also encouraged by her father, who would raid the Party Pieces fancy-dress stock and dress up every Christmas – including one year as a sumo wrestler. Both Kate and William opted for a fancy-dress theme for their parties. Kate chose the elegant and dramatic flair of the 1920s and wore a stunning flapper dress for the champagne reception at her parents' home in June. William slipped in to the party after the other guests had arrived.

Later in the month it was William's turn to celebrate, although his party was held in Windsor Castle and saw the Queen dressed as the Queen of Swaziland in a glittering white gown and African headdress. William had first been to Africa in 1998 with Prince Harry and their family friends the van Cutsems, and he had returned during his gap year – his passion for the country prompted his decision to make his theme Out of Africa. The whole venue was decorated to look like the African jungle, with huge model elephants in the corners, tribal masks on the walls and a lifelike replica giraffe's head above the bar, while a band called Shakarimba were flown over from Botswana, and William took to the stage to play drums.

Headlines the next day were mainly about Aaron Barschak – the self-styled comedy terrorist who gatecrashed dressed as Osama bin Laden, and who leaped onstage in the middle of William's speech and grabbed the microphone, before being hauled off. It was also noted that sitting next to William was his old flame, Jecca Craig. She was the daughter of conservationist Ian Craig, and William had been linked to her when he stayed with the family on his gap year. However, in an interview he gave the Press Association to commemorate his twenty-first birthday, he stated that he didn't have a 'steady girlfriend', explaining: 'If I fancy a girl and I really like her and she fancies me back, which is rare, I ask her out. But, at the same time, I don't want to put them in an awkward situation because a lot of people don't quite understand what comes with knowing me, for one, and secondly, if they were my girlfriend, the excitement it would probably cause.' He knew that he and Kate needed to take their time.

When they returned to St Andrews in September 2003 for the beginning of their third year, their families knew that William and Kate were together and Kate had met Prince Charles. It was clear to the couple that they had something good, and something that could last. They were not only drawn together by their similarities, but also by supporting each other. While Kate had been a rock for William when his great-grandmother and best friend's brother had died, William was there for Kate this next year when her first grandparent – her mother's father Ron – passed away.

The couple had moved out from Hope Street to a more private residence called Balgove House, which stood on the Strathtyrum Estate, belonging to Henry Cheape, a friend of the royal family. Fergus and Olivia had decided to stay on in Hope Street, so for their remaining two years, Kate and William lived with two of their other close friends Oli Baker and Alasdair Coutts-Wood.

It was quite a different arrangement to their previous flat, but the bulletproof windows, bombproof door and security system were all in place. Their new home was a four-bedroomed cottage located a quarter of a mile outside town, hidden up a long gravel drive lined with fruit trees and set in two acres of wild grassland. Inside was a small sitting room with an open fire on the right and a large kitchen-diner with black-and-white chequered floor on the left. The kitchen was fitted with an Aga, and in the dining room was a vast mahogany dining table that could seat around twenty, with a battered oil painting of the Queen and a Union flag on the wall. William set about installing a champagne fridge, while Kate dressed the windows with red-and-white gingham curtains.

The foursome went out into town less and did more hosting at home, Kate roasted the venison that William had shot and they drank inexpensive wine. During parties, they kept the beers cold in the porcelain bath filled with ice. The house also gave them an idyllic haven of private pastures to enjoy. The grounds were full of crab apple trees, wild poppies and rioting tangles of rhododendrons – they would have picnics stretched out on a blanket with a chilled bottle of wine, or light a barbecue in the fire pit. It was secret, romantic and relaxed. Kate and William both had cars at university, and at weekends they would sometimes make the seventy-five-mile journey to the Queen's home at Balmoral in the Scottish Highlands. They wouldn't stay in the big house, however, but in one of the other smaller and cosier homes scattered across the vast estate.

Prince Albert had bought Balmoral for Queen Victoria and the land was gradually added to, so that the medieval-style grey-stone castle now lies in a vast 50,000 acres of moors and woodland. One of the properties they stayed in was Birkhall, which belongs to Prince Charles and where he spends time every year. It was previously the Queen Mother's residence on the estate. Charles had spent his own money on renovations since he took on the tenancy; however, he kept the Queen

Mother's beloved and worn tartan curtains, much to Camilla's amusement and dismay.

Later, Kate and William would stay in Tam-na-Ghar a 120-year-old cottage with three bedrooms, which the Queen allowed William to use. At this point it was given a £150,000 renovation, and Prince Harry was also given a set of keys but, of course, he had much less use for it as he wasn't based in Scotland. The couple were able to enjoy the cottage as a romantic getaway set in acres of heather moors, where they could enjoy a roaring log fire, a bottle of red wine and cook their own meals. They would make the most of the rolling miles of wild terrain laced through with streams and brooks, and thickly wooded with Caledonian pines. They could go deer stalking or salmon fishing in the River Dee, which cuts through the land, or take morning walks in the mist.

Kate already knew how to handle a gun as she had been taking lessons at her local shooting school in Berkshire. She and the rest of her family had received tuition on more than one occasion, where they were taught how to shoot clay pigeons as well as gun-handling and gun-safety.

On other weekends, they would visit friend's family homes on the east coast of Scotland and in the Highlands or they would go to small properties on the Sandringham estate or to the Scottish ski resort of Aviemore.

At a friend's twenty-first birthday party, it was clear that Kate was still getting used to William's public role. The pair attended a *Gone With the Wind*-themed party at a castle and there was no expense spared. Guests all wore black tie and the party area was decorated with giant replica oil paintings and golden ornaments in keeping with the grand theme. 'Will was dancing with the birthday girl's mum and asking about her grandmother,' recalls Michael Choong, who also attended. 'They loved him and he knew what to say to them. I think everyone realized, including Kate, that she wasn't part of a normal relationship. Will had his duties and other priorities, which any potential partner would have to accommodate.'

By this point, some who knew them both had remarked that Kate seemed to perhaps be losing her identity. It was natural in a new relationship to tumble headlong into the giddy joy of it, spending lots of time together, and wanting to be a big part of each others' lives, but added to that were William's unique circumstances. It was inevitable that Kate would need to fit to him more than he would have to fit to her, so she inevitably needed to make more compromises and sacrifices. She became closer to his group of friends, and the friends they made together. In some ways, they were just another couple of university students, studying, socializing and falling in love, but what William and the rest of the royal family considered as 'normal' was still not normal by most other people's standards.

William's station made it impossible for things to be as Kate had been used to in the first two decades of her life, and she had to make allowances because of who he was. She would need to be careful about whom she spoke to and what she said to them. Her actions and behaviour could be misinterpreted and be reported on – and this was not what she was used to. It was quite a turnaround for the strong, self-assured girl who was smart, and had so many of her own interests, passions and aspirations. She was still only twenty-one and going through a period of readjustment, while dealing with some extraordinary circumstances.

William was more independent at this stage and wanted to

remain that way for a while to come. When the world is at your feet, do you want to settle down forever at the age of twenty-one? Kate found the answer was, no.

CHAPTER SIX

Front-page news

Despite being surrounded by a campus full of students, and with the press – even from a distance – forever watching, Kate and William had been together for a year before their relationship became public knowledge. It all changed when they took a skiing holiday together in the luxury Swiss resort of Klosters, where at one point they held hands around Kate's ski pole. The couple were being observed by paparazzo Jason Fraser, who seven years earlier had snapped the first picture of William's mother Diana with her new boyfriend Dodi Al Fayed, proving publicly that they were in a relationship.

Kate and William's hand-holding was the sign that the press had been waiting for, and the following day the picture was splashed across the front page of the *Sun*, alongside the headline, 'Finally … Wills gets a girl.' The pair had flown to the royals' favourite resort in April 2004 for a spring break with Prince

Harry, the princes' mutual friends Thomas van Straubenzee and Guy Pelly, and William and Harry's former nanny turned friend Tiggy Pettifer. The fact that Kate and William weren't there with mutual friends from St Andrews, but with William's brother and some their oldest friends, was significant in showing how close the couple had become, and how serious they were about each other. For the photographer, the romantic snowy backdrop was a bonus.

Despite having been Prince Charles's favourite ski resort for decades – one of the cable cars is even called the 'Prince Charles'– the famous locale is set around a simple Swiss village with just a few hotels and chalets tucked away in the woods. It's traditional but also luxurious. Kate's school ski trips had set her in good stead, and she was accomplished on the slopes; in fact, William even conceded later, 'She's better than me at tennis and skiing but I'm better at everything else!'

Wearing red-and-black mix-and-match ski gear, the pair hit the slopes, and because they were used to pretty much being left alone and they were among friends and family, they were tactile and unguarded. The picture seen around the world was a happy one in which they looked like any other young couple in love, grinning at each other and holding hands. However, because of the press agreement that was made when William first went to St Andrews that he would be left alone for the four-year span of his course, the royal family was not happy. The *Sun* argued that he was the future king and if he was in a significant relationship then it was in the public's interest to know. Both sides moved on from the incident, cautiously.

However, just two months later, by the time they broke for summer, Kate and William were also on a break from their relationship. They were both still only twenty-two and had another year at university to go, let alone thinking about the long-term future. Many St Andrews students concur that though the town is perfect for building a strong and supportive student community, because it is so small, by the time they are reaching the three-year mark they start to feel the confines of an intimate environment. They are cut off from the non-student life that they know will embrace them soon and, seeing the same faces everywhere, they begin to feel a yearning for life beyond the tiny town. William was also feeling the confines of being in a relationship, and he and Kate decided to spend some time apart. This was the first serious relationship for both of them, so they had nothing to compare it to and were finding their feet as they went along.

Kate decided to take on some work over the summer, and when she returned home to Bucklebury, she approached the clothing shop at her local shooting school about opportunities. She had been a regular visitor at the school for some time, taking clay-pigeon-shooting lessons and learning about gun-handling and gun-safety along with some of her family. She had discovered the luxury brand Really Wild Clothing in the shop that was based there, and the designs suited her – a mixture of classic country style with a modern urban edge. 'She came into the shop to ask if there was perhaps a position, or some work she could do over the summer,' recalls Sara Johnson-Watts, who has worked alongside designer Natalie Lake to develop the brand over the years. 'Kate had shooting tuition over the previous years so she was quite familiar with several members of staff and felt comfortable enquiring about opportunities.'

It was perfect timing for Really Wild, as they were launching their new collection countrywide at the nearby Blenheim Game Fair, and took Kate on for a few days' promotional work. 'She walked into it saying she would do whatever was required,' recalls Sara. 'She was quite a bit younger than the rest of us, but she was very mature and took on various roles throughout the day. We didn't really need to explain anything, she just hit the right note. She helped customers try things on, put things in bags, handed out leaflets, it was very low-key, and she was such a joy to have around.'

The news of Kate and William's relationship had been broken in the papers just a few months earlier, and although by then they were taking some time apart, it wasn't public knowledge and there was inevitable interest in her when people at the fair realized who she was. 'There was quite a bit of interest that descended on the stand,' Sara explains. 'To protect her, we did suggest she didn't help us on the second day, as there was so much attention directed towards her. However, she said: "No, no, I gave you my word and I'll be there." She was just a complete star.'

William spent the summer break enjoying holidays and hanging out with friends. He first headed to Nashville, Tennessee, with a few friends to stay at the family home of fellow St Andrews student, Anna Sloan, and then he embarked on a boys' sailing trip to Greece, where the boat was staffed with an all-female crew. William also expressed an interest in aristocratic actress Isabella Anstruther-Gough-Calthorpe, whose brother, Jacobi, he knew from playing polo. The willowy blonde had just played her first big screen role in the Claire Danes' film *Stage Beauty*, and went on to marry Virgin heir Sam Branson. Although she rebuffed William they remained friends, and not only did she attend the royal wedding but Prince Harry ended up in a relationship with her half-sister, Cressida Bonas.

In the meantime, Kate spent her free time in the summer of 2004 with her family in Bucklebury and holidaying in the Dordogne, South of France, at the family home of hers and William's old housemate, Fergus Boyd. Other friends who were there included another former housemate, Olivia Bleasdale, and good friend Ginny Fraser. Kate was out of sorts and, one evening, after a few glasses of wine, said she was missing William.

But as the summer progressed, it seemed that two months apart was as much as the couple could take. By August, the pair were back on track. William took Kate to the beautiful island of Rodrigues in the Indian Ocean, which is where he had spent some of his gap year. It was also where he decided to base his final-year university thesis, studying the erosion of the coral reef. Rodrigues is a simple, tropical paradise with a lush-green landscape and little houses with corrugated rooftops. At night, with no light pollution, the starry skies seem to go on forever. It was the first time they had been to the Indian Ocean together, but it wasn't to be the last.

Back in Scotland and bracing themselves for winter, the pair committed themselves to their fourth and final year of studies. Kate wasn't sure what she would be doing next. There were many avenues open to her, but she didn't need to think about that just yet. For now, her energy was taken up with her dissertation, which was on the author of *Alice in Wonderland* and entitled, '"Angels from Heaven": Lewis Carroll's Photographic Interpretation of Childhood'. William knew that after university his life would never be the same as he would be taking on a certain amount of royal duties, and he still had a lot to learn. He would need to spend some time in the armed forces, and would be undertaking assorted work experience.

In November 2004, Kate attended Prince Charles's fifty-sixth birthday celebrations, which, despite the blip over the summer, showed already how close she was to her boyfriend's father, and how well he thought of her. Further proof that she had been embraced by William's family came when she was also invited on Charles's 'stag weekend' the following spring. The Prince of Wales was set to marry the woman he had first fallen in love with thirty-four years earlier, and he took a small group away with him for a skiing trip to Klosters before the wedding.

It was the day some thought would never come. When Charles first met Camilla Shand, she was twenty-three and he was twenty-two. Although he was immediately taken with her and they became something of an item, his military career was just beginning, and the young prince was also keen to make the most of single life before duty called. He simply wasn't sure he wanted to settle down at such a young age. Three years later, while he was away at sea, Camilla, who by that time *was* ready to settle down, got engaged to her former boyfriend, Andrew Parker Bowles. But Camilla and Charles's friendship never ended

When Charles had been seeing Lady Diana Spencer for four months and the press found out, his father the Duke of Edinburgh urged him to make his mind up as to whether Diana was a long-term prospect or a fun fling as, now the relationship was public, it would affect her reputation. Charles took this to mean that he should be moving forward in his relationship with Diana and decided to propose.

Although an undefined friendship between Charles and Camilla continued throughout the first few years of his marriage to Diana, it certainly became a relationship again in 1984, around the time that Diana started a relationship with

James Hewitt. Camilla was divorced in 1995 and, following his divorce in 1997, Charles had been just about to start introducing Camilla as his partner in an official capacity, when Diana died. Around a year later, William and Harry met Camilla for the first time. Although relations were understandably difficult to begin with, both boys realized that she made their father happy, and they have grown very fond of her in the ensuing years. Publicly, Charles and Camilla first appeared side by side together in January 1999, when they left the Ritz Hotel following a party for Camilla's sister. By the time they reached their wedding day they had been together, the second time around, for over twenty years.

Although Kate wasn't invited to the wedding, as she wasn't a member of the royal family yet, she could certainly be there for the informal personal celebrations when Charles took his small party to Klosters. Like the year before on the same slopes, the trip was another of firsts – Kate was photographed with Charles for the first time when they rode a gondola together, and William and Kate were also photographed hugging in public for the first time. Despite being a trip organized by the fifty-six-year-old prince, it was a raucous fun holiday as well, thanks to the presence of William and Harry and some of their friends. The Casa Antica nightclub has long been a favourite with British visitors, including the royal party, and is set over three floors, with a chill-out bar on one, a piano bar on another, and a throbbing DJ set on the third. It has been described as a mansion taken over by eccentric sixties hipsters, and 'a relaxed jeans kind of place with the odd stag's head thrown in'. One night, the young party were in high spirits and the princes' friend Guy Pelly ran into the bar wearing just his boxer shorts, and sat on one male customer's lap. Prince William then informed Guy that the man was actually the new royal correspondent for the *Sun*.

As Guy sloped off, William called the reporter over, who duly asked if William was going to get married any time soon, which is when he gave the quote which would follow him for the next six years: 'Look, I'm only twenty-two for God's sake. I'm too young to marry at my age. I don't want to get married until I'm at least twenty-eight or maybe thirty.'

Kate was just as involved with the high jinks of the night as the two brothers and their friends, and as the others tussled with Harry, his beaded bracelet, which was a present from his girlfriend Chelsy Davy, was torn off, and he was left scrabbling round on the floor trying to pick the beads up. They then proceeded to try to pull his jeans down to prove he was 'going commando'.

Back at St Andrews, just as everyone was beginning to think they knew Kate, she surprised them again, this time when she auditioned for the St Andrews drama society's final-year performance of *My Fair Lady*. 'She just pitched up after four years, where no one knew she was dramatic or musical at all,' explains Michael Choong. 'She didn't seem outgoing in that way at all. I found that so curious. She told me she had played Eliza at school, but she didn't get the part this time.'

Although she and William had been through their first rocky patch, things were now good between them. After celebrating the end of exams by being soaked with shaken up cans of fizzy drinks, in June came another first, when Kate and William attended their first society wedding together. William's childhood friend Hugh van Cutsem was marrying Rose Astor, and although Kate and William didn't arrive together, the fact they were both there was significant. Wearing a white fitted jacket over a black-and-white lace dress with a black fascinator on the side of her head, it was a classic wedding look that Kate would become famous for over the coming years as their friends all started getting married.

After they celebrated William's twenty-third birthday together at the Beaufort Polo Club, it was time to leave St Andrews. It was the place that had seen them go from first blushing introduction, to easy friends, close confidantes and a couple in love. They had broken up and made up, and the small city had been their home for four years, protecting them, seeing them make friends for life and giving them the last prolonged period of normality they would ever have. So it was a bittersweet experience as they reached graduation day.

On 23 June 2005, dressed in a crisp white shirt, black miniskirt and heels, Kate graduated St Andrews with an upper second-class degree in History of Art. William Wales received an upper second in Geography. Although the oldest part of the university dates back to the fifteenth century, the Younger Hall where they graduated was surprisingly contemporary and functional, having been built in the 1930s. After a morning chapel service, they headed there to receive their degrees. It was also where not only the Middletons were seated for their daughter's big day, but Charles and Camilla, the Queen and the Duke of Edinburgh. Kate had not yet met the Queen, and did not meet her that day. It was a time for the couple to celebrate together with all their friends and family, rather than ducking off for a brief and private first meeting. However, Charles and Camilla had invited the Middletons for dinner the night before, which is when they met each other for the first time. At the end of the ceremony,

Vice Chancellor Dr Brian Lang said, 'You will have made life-long friends. You may have met your husband or wife. Our title as the top matchmaking university in Britain signifies so much that is good about St Andrews, we rely on you to go forth and multiply.'

For both Kate and William, the safe bubble of life at university was burst, and things would never be the same again. Like many university graduates, Kate hadn't yet worked out what she wanted to do next. She was also, however, in the unique position whereby, even if she and William didn't end up together, she was still required to behave in a certain way while she was his significant partner. This would, understandably, affect her decision-making process, and would have some bearing on what she did next.

For Kate, even if she wasn't ready to think about the long-term future of her relationship with William at that point, she still needed to at least seriously consider that eventuality. She might end up as her boyfriend's queen, or she might end up as her boyfriend's subject. She was in a unique and tricky position at a time when there was already so much to try to decide upon.

Leaving St Andrews was perhaps an even more dramatic and significant change for William, as his immediate future was being mapped out in preparation for a job that was his destiny. He was coming to terms with his own dilemmas, questions and a strong sense of inevitability. Additionally, as they left the small coastal town, the press agreement was lifted and it left them both exposed.

CHAPTER SEVEN

'He wants more than anything for it to stop'

As William was advised and guided by a crack team of experts who helped him plan the next eighteen months, Kate chatted to friends and family about her options – should she try to use her degree in some way and apply for jobs in galleries? Or should she look into setting up her own business in a similar vein to her parents? That summer, after graduation, William – representing the Queen – visited New Zealand to commemorate the sixtieth anniversary of the end of the Second World War. There he undertook many personal royal firsts, including taking a royal salute as troops marched past, inspecting a guard of honour, planting a tree and going on a solo walkabout. They were all to be key parts of his public royal duties and showed how swiftly he was becoming more involved in royal life now he had left university.

Afterwards, Kate and William headed to Kenya. It was Kate's first time in Africa – the country that had captured William's heart since he first visited as a sixteen-year-old. They were joined by a few friends and they spent some time with his old friends the Craigs at their home. He had stayed with them on their 61,000-acre reserve, the Lewa Wildlife Conservancy, on his first visit. Elephants and black rhino had been decimated by poachers and the Craigs had turned their entire reserve over to house a rhino sanctuary.

Then, they travelled on to the Il Ngwesi Lodge in the Mukogodo Hills, Northern Kenya. The eco lodge is built from locally sourced materials and looks like it has simply bloomed from the hillside rather than actually being built – with wooden stilts and a grassy canopy, and most of the inside crafted from wood. The outdoors shower has a view of the surrounding bush, and the saltwater infinity pool overlooks a watering hole that was often teeming with elephants. They ate outdoors and celebrated their graduation, enjoying their last holiday before working life beckoned.

Back in London, Kate was based in the Chelsea flat her parents had bought. Located in a quiet tree-lined street just off the Kings Road, it afforded her the best of both worlds. She was slightly tucked away from all the action, but had shops, restaurants, clubs and cafes on her doorstep. However, she was missing the one thing that had meant home to her for the past three years – William. He was about to embark on six months of work experience, followed by years of military training, which meant they would be not only no longer living under the same roof, but often would be in different cities. William's official base was at his father's residence in Clarence House, into which Prince Charles, William and Harry had moved after the previous resident, the Queen Mother, had died. William and Harry had their own apartments there, and it was where their home was whenever they were in London. Kate and William had been used to waking up together every morning for the past three years, and although they spent a lot of time together in Kate's Chelsea flat and in Clarence House, it was different from what they were used to. They were no longer living together. However they both had work to do, and that was the priority at the time.

It was a period of adjustment for Kate. She was going for job interviews and getting used to living in London, as well as getting used to the attention she was now receiving. After growing up in the countryside, and then going to a small university town where everyone knew each other, she was now living in the sprawling, brawling metropolis. London is so vast it often takes more than an hour to travel from one part of the city to another: it is loud, fast and in-your-face. Additionally, the press agreement concerning leaving William alone had been lifted so not only was he now pursued and photographed, but so was Kate. Because she was living in the capital, it wasn't long before the paparazzi had worked out where she lived and they were often camped outside her flat. She was beginning to pose something of a conundrum.

As the long-term girlfriend of the second in line to the throne, she was inevitably going to command a great deal of interest, especially as she was young and attractive. However, she was not royalty herself, and so she had no security, and no official mouthpiece. She handled it well, and kept smiling. Panic buttons had already been installed in her flat, so that if a situation became threatening, she would have assistance immediately. As for not having an official mouthpiece, she handled certain things herself with aplomb. When she attended the Gatcombe Park Horse Trials and a photographer asked her to pose for a picture, she told him no, politely but firmly: 'If I do it now I'll have to keep doing it at skiing or every time!' The photographer told her she looked beautiful and she blushed, but she had asserted herself. For a young woman of twenty-three she was handling herself very well.

In October, however, she was photographed on a bus while going for a job interview. It was argued that there was no difference being photographed on the bus, than from being photographed walking down the street or shopping with her mother, but the big difference in this instance was that Kate had been followed by the photographer all day. On instructions from William, who had discussed the matter with Kate and her father, a legal letter to newspaper editors was issued requesting that details of Kate's private life remain private. William had a life-long mistrust of the paparazzi, and even began to do his own research into complex privacy laws to work out how best to protect his girlfriend. She had some of the best first-hand advice on how to deal with the press and public from William, and she also had training from Charles's advisors, which included watching footage of Diana to see how she had coped with the paparazzi. Kate continued to use the bus and underground to travel around London, and William also gave her his black VW, which she used to drive back home to see her parents.

She threw herself into the bright lights, big city life. Her new home was just off one of London's busiest and most upmarket shopping thoroughfares. The Kings Road was like a catwalk, where people didn't just pop to the shops, but swept around them with year-round tans, full makeup and a great deal of camel-coloured cashmere. Her own style was changing, but

Above: Young Kate with her mother Carole at a friend's first birthday party, January 1983.

Right: Prince William with his mother Diana, Princess of Wales, in February 1983.

Above: At Uncle Gary's first wedding in 1992, Kate (*left*), Pippa and James pose with their parents Michael and Carole and maternal grandparents Ron and Dorothy.

Right: Young Prince William (*seated, right*) with his family in 1992.

Above: Kate (*front row, centre*) in the hockey team at St Andrew's School. Always sporty, she also took part in netball, tennis and swimming among other sports.

Below: After an unpleasant experience at all girls' boarding school Downe House, Kate (*right*) was much happier at Marlborough College.

Above: In 2001 Kate (*far right*) took part in a Raleigh International Expedition to Patagonia, Chile, little knowing that her future husband had been to Chile with Raleigh just ten weeks earlier.

Right: The couple got together at university, but it wasn't until 2006 that they were first photographed kissing in public, here at the Eton Field Game.

Above: Kate with her parents, Michael and Carole, at Sandhurst Military Academy for William's 'passing out' in December 2006.

Left: By March 2007 it was apparent that not all was well in the relationship, which led the couple to split the following month.

Left: Kate and Pippa Middleton – the Sizzler Sisters – arriving at a book launch in May 2007.

Right: Enjoying a lighter moment with Prince Harry and Camilla, Duchess of Cornwall, at the ceremony at which William was installed as a Knight of the Garter in 2008.

or their first official engagement together, Kate and William launched a lifeboat at rearddur Bay RNLI Lifeboat Station, Anglesey, in February 2011.

Far left: Kate in 2006; (*left*) by 2008 she had blossomed into a style icon.

Below: Kate, woman about town, turning heads in the Kings Road, Chelsea just days before her wedding in April 2011.

she was yet to evolve into the fashion icon of later years. While at university she favoured boot-cut jeans with sweaters and shirts and air-dried hair, she smartened up for the city and the inevitable job interviews. But as she was finding which clothes worked best for her, for a while it was noted she dressed a little old for her twenty-three years, in tailored jackets and knotted pashminas, or mumsy florals. She had, however, been introduced to the Richard Ward Salon by her mother, and would go for blow-dries and manicures – often with her mum and sister. Kate always opted for a simple but effective look, with shine-boosting glossing treatments and big bouncy blow-dries. Her stylist was James Pryce and he was the trusted favourite who later went on to style her wedding day hair and accompany her on her first royal tour across Canada. When Pippa visited on a break from Edinburgh University, they would also go to the popular Bluebird restaurant.

William spent his time undertaking assorted work-experience assignments that were set up to help him understand some key areas of business in the country over which he would one day reign. He learned how to run a country estate when he stayed with the Duke and Duchess of Devonshire on their Chatsworth Estate for two weeks. While he was there, he helped deliver a calf, drove tractors and worked in the butchers. He then spent three weeks working at HSBC headquarters, in the charity services division, followed by a stint at the Bank of England, and at the queen's solicitors Farrer and Co, the London Stock Exchange, Lloyd's of London and the Financial Services Authority. He also spent a few weeks in Anglesey, North Wales, with the RAF Valley Mountain Rescue Team, which certainly struck a chord with him, as it was to be where he would return to work after his RAF training four years later.

He returned to London frequently, and he and Kate would make the most of their new life in the capital. Many of the clubs they frequented with their friends and siblings were expensive, popular and interchangeable. They were simply a place to drink, dance and bump up against others. Dark, smoky places throbbing with loud music and packed with similarly pretty people who were all dressed up, and knew exactly where to go. They would drink vodka cranberries in the likes of Mamilanji with its bar, lounge and club linked by marble corridors, or two-floor celebrity-packed club Embassy. Other passing favourites included Purple, which was located in the Chelsea football grounds and thus impossible for paps to get in to, and Raffles, which has a light-up dance floor and a central podium with a pillar just asking for amateur pole-dancers to give it a whirl. For a more sedate evening, Kate and William would head off on their own for a bite to eat at the Pigs Ear, an award-winning gastro-pub with a meat-heavy menu that included the titular salted crispy pig's ear.

As the year came to a close, a German magazine printed a photograph of William leaving Kate's flat, which clearly showed where she lived. It was hugely irresponsible, and meant that afterwards the couple would mostly stay at William's apartments in Clarence House.

Knowing that they wouldn't be spending much time together over the next few months, Kate and William made the most of the festive break and Kate was invited to Sandringham on Boxing Day for the family's traditional pheasant shoot. She and William stayed on there afterwards – moving to one of the smaller properties on the estate to celebrate New Year's Eve together. In January 2006, Kate celebrated her twenty-fourth birthday with friends and family, but not William. Two days earlier, he had left to enrol in the Army at Sandhurst military academy, where he would be based for the next year.

It is a requirement for all male members of the royal family to train in the armed forces. Since their job description will forever be to serve their country, this is literally what their military training is about. Prince Charles and Prince Andrew had served in the Navy, and Prince Edward in the Royal Marines. Harry had skipped university and after his gap year had gone straight to Sandhurst, so he was already on his way.

William had a hard slog ahead of him, with 5 a.m. starts and eighteen-hour days to look forward to. Additionally, no laptops or phones were allowed for the first five weeks. It was also difficult for Kate, as she wouldn't see her boyfriend again for his first five weeks of training when he would be on lockdown. He was starting out on a military commitment that would continue for the rest of his life.

It was clear to the outside world exactly how William was spending his time, as announcements were made by his team to the press. Kate was not a member of the royal family, and so was leading a private life with no press statements accounting for her movements. As soon as she set foot in the street she was followed by paparazzi and written about in the papers, but no one knew what she was doing behind closed doors, no one knew what work she was undertaking. In time, questions were asked about how she was making a living or if she was earning at all.

She was in fact working for her parents' company Party Pieces, but unless she herself was to inform the press about it, it of course went unreported. She was a blank sheet of paper, and people began to doodle what they wanted on to it. She was in a difficult position, however, since if she spoke to the press she would have been seen as an attention seeker who felt the need to justify herself, and if she didn't it was assumed she was doing nothing. She wisely chose the latter course and bit her tongue.

If someone is so closely connected to the royal family, the best course of action is to take on the royal code of conduct just to be on the safe side, which has always been: 'Don't complain, don't explain.' So in pap pictures, she was always smiling, always good tempered and quietly going about her life. The only time she has spoken about the matter of what she did for work was during her engagement interview when she said, 'I know I've been working very hard for the family business, sometimes those days are long days ... if I'm pulling my weight, everyone who I work with can see I'm pulling my weight and that's what matters to me.'

All three Middleton children have worked for their parents at one time or another – while some families produce generations of lawyers, doctors or podiatrists, the Middletons' forte is capitalizing on celebrating creatively. It isn't as easily recognizable a job description as a lawyer, but they are good at it, and it works for them. Kate worked on marketing the company, putting the catalogue together and taking a course on web design so that she could make more of the business's online presence.

She was also moving slowly and carefully into royal life. Key occasions in the royal calendar include assorted horse-related events, and one of the earliest in the year is the Cheltenham Gold Cup in March – a key race in the Cheltenham Festival. In 2006, Kate attended with a friend, but was then invited into the royal box for lunch with Charles and Camilla, which was telling because William wasn't there and so she was clearly being accepted as one of the family. Additionally, it was the first time she had been seen in public with Charles and Camilla in a formal setting. She later watched the races with Camilla's children Tom and Laura Parker Bowles and William's best friend Thomas van Straubenzee.

Other firsts swiftly followed. In May, she and William went to the wedding of Camilla's daughter Laura Parker Bowles to Harry Lopes, which was their first family wedding together. Around this time, Charles also gave his permission for them to sleep in the same bed when they stayed over at his country home, Highgrove. Throughout the year, when William was on leave he would also spend many weekends at the Middletons' home, getting to know Kate's family better.

After the initial gruelling five weeks at Sandhurst, Kate and William made up for lost time by taking a trip to the Caribbean island Mustique, and they were loaned Villa Hibiscus by Belle and John Robinson who own the Jigsaw clothing-store chain. William had negotiated the stay with the couple, who offered him their villa for free, so he instead made a donation to a hospital on the neighbouring island of St Vincent. The villa was all they had hoped for – set in the hillside overlooking Macaroni Beach, with views of other Caribbean islands, they played volleyball and took on the islanders at frisbee. They also met up with their friends Holly and Sam Branson's father – Virgin tycoon Richard Branson – for tennis. They visited a guesthouse called Firefly for cocktails where William drank vodka cranberry and Kate sipped pina coladas. As well as having a dream holiday, the link with the Jigsaw owners also led to a career opportunity for Kate, which she would pursue when she returned home.

Jigsaw would be a perfect fit for Kate, who could have been a poster girl for the label. She had cast off her university wardrobe and refined her initial ageing London look, and was becoming known for her flirty feminine style. She teamed skinny jeans with pretty tops and floaty sundresses with French Sole pumps. That summer was the first flash of even more to come in the style stakes. When she attended the first of what were to become a glamorous biennial amateur charity event, the Boodles Boxing Ball, she sizzled in a floor-length azure satin BCBG Max Azria gown. It was slashed down the front, with crisscrossed ribbons accenting her tiny waist, and she accessorized it with a deep golden tan. It was the kind of style which had never been associated with Kate before, but it was clear that with this look she had become one to watch. Kate and William were still cutting a dash through the London social scene whenever he was visiting. Along with Prince Harry, his girlfriend Chelsy Davy and their friends, the pair enjoyed the razzle-dazzle of life in the capital.

After flitting around a number of clubs when they first started socializing in London, Kate and William had now found their favourites – upscale clubs Boujis and Mahiki. At private-members club Boujis, membership started at £500 a year and prospective chosen ones also had to know a member in order to join. The royal party was there so often that in 2006 the owner instated the 'royal comp', where bar-bills would be waived for the princes because they and their party brought such immeasurable publicity to the club. Boujis was purple-lit with a decadent feel. Miniature bulbs studded the ceiling and long booths dotted with silver ice buckets of champagne and vodka lined the walls. The club's signature drink was the 'Crack Baby' – vodka and passion fruit juice topped with champagne and served in a test tube – and all the royal party drank them. They would usually head down on Tuesday nights and would be shown into the brown room, one of the suede lined VIP rooms. Thursdays was usually reserved for Mahiki, which was more of a fun party place modelled on a Polynesian beach bar, with bamboo screens, revolving retro ceiling fans and a Fijian war canoe hung over the bar. Customers drank cocktails out of coconuts, and the most famous creation was the Treasure Chest – which was served in a wooden chest and comprised brandy, peach liqueur, lime and sugar, topped with a bottle of Moet & Chandon champagne and cost upwards of £100.

It wasn't long, however, before reality cast a shadow over Kate's new life, when she had to deal with the loss of both her grandmothers within two months. It was a huge blow to her close-knit family. Firstly, in July, Carole's mother Dorothy succumbed to cancer at the age of seventy-one. Carole had been close to her mother and they not only looked alike, but had the same drive and aspirations that saw them make the best of their lives. Kate read a poem at the funeral, which was attended by villager Dudley Singleton, who remembered, 'The last time I saw Kate was at her grandmother's funeral. A wake was held in a marquee, not only for family but also for all the friends she had made in the village. Everyone was invited back to the house.'

Shortly after her mother's funeral, Carole asked her brother Gary if she could bring her family to his villa in Ibiza to get away from it all. It was the perfect spot to escape to – named La Maison de Bang Bang, it was completely private and overlooked the sea, and they could sit out by the pool, soak up the sun and enjoy some family meals together.

William came out to join them on their last weekend, and they went sailing on a yacht, visiting a local island with mud baths where they rolled in the healing mud. One of Gary's friends also taught William how to DJ on his mixing decks. It was a brief respite from the family's loss, however, as just two weeks later, Michael's mother Valerie died from lymphoma at the age of eighty-two.

Shortly afterwards, Kate started her new job, working for Jigsaw as an accessories buyer. 'People assumed it was a mercy act on our part,' Belle Robinson told the *Evening Standard*. 'But Kate's a bright girl. She set up the website for her parents' business so we thought those skills would be useful.' Every day Kate drove to the offices in Kew in her new silver Audi, and she would travel the country going to fairs to get inspiration. Additionally, she co-designed a charm necklace while she was there – a fine silver chain hung with a silver bean, rose quartz crystal and pink freshwater pearl. The necklaces sold for £57 each, and were created with jewellery designer Claudia Bradby. She was the wife of ITV political correspondent Tom Bradby, who had struck up a friendship with Prince William when he filmed him during his gap year and who later conducted Kate and William's engagement interview.

Kate had been dubbed 'Waity Katie' in the press, as it seemed that she was simply waiting around for William to propose. She quite rightly hated the title. Privately, she was prepared to wait, because she knew they had something good, and she knew he had duties to fulfil, but in her working life it was harder. She didn't have a vocational degree and so didn't have one set job in mind that would be perfect for her. Many twenty-somethings with humanities degrees experiment with different careers, but she was criticized for seeming unsure of what she wanted to so and trying out a few different paths. She needed to be careful though – while she was in a relationship with William, she couldn't been seen to be using her royal connections to further her career, and so she had to choose well. The Middletons had already being accused of using their royal association to boost their business, and it was something that Sophie, Countess of Wessex, had discovered during her relationship with Prince Edward. When they met, Sophie had her own PR company, but she was accused of using her royal connections in her business dealings, and after her marriage she quit her job to work as a full-time royal. So Kate was treading lightly while trying out the fashion industry as a possible career.

As 2006 came to an end, there came another very noticeable milestone in Kate and William's relationship. The couple had spent a lot of time with each other's family, but William's passing-out ceremony at Sandhurst was the first formal occasion where they would all be in attendance. Charles and Diana's courtship was so short that the matter of her family being involved in a royal occasion didn't need to be addressed, but even after they were married there wasn't much crossover between the Windsors and the Spencers.

Things had changed a great deal in two decades, and William had always been close to Kate's parents. So when he graduated from Sandhurst, he invited not only his girlfriend, but her family as well. Additionally, the Middletons didn't walk through the car park like the other families – they walked the red carpet as did the Queen, Prince Philip, Charles and Camilla. Although the Queen attended, it still wasn't the time for her and Kate to meet. Just like the graduation at St Andrews, this was a day for William to celebrate with his contemporaries, rather than disappear with his grandmother and girlfriend and their families.

Kate turned heads as the usually demurely-dressed twenty-four-year-old wore a scarlet Armani coat revealing a black lace-trimmed vest teamed with black leather gloves with cut-outs. Lip readers hired by ITV reported that when she saw William, she said to her mum, 'I love the uniform, so sexy.' William wore his No. 1 dress – navy-blue tunic and trousers, with a red stripe down the leg, red sash and navy hat with a red band. He tried not to smile as the Queen carried out an inspection.

It was also commented on that Carole broke with protocol by chewing gum during the ceremony, although it was later revealed that it was nicotine gum as she was trying to give up smoking. It wasn't the first time that Kate and her family had been on the ugly end of snobbery. Some palace courtiers and associates of William, who should have known better in these supposedly enlightened times, spoke about her behind her back. To some, Kate was seen as not blue-blooded enough to marry a prince and be a future queen, and when she turned up to certain events, there were snide comments of 'doors to manual' in reference to her mother's former career. Kate was aware of the bitchy comments that were being made, but had the good sense to ignore them.

Additionally, Pippa, studying at Edinburgh University, was also on the gossip radar. She was dating and hanging out with aristocrats and she and Kate had been acidly dubbed the 'wisteria sisters' by *Tatler* magazine because, according to the society bible, they were 'highly decorative, terribly fragrant and have a ferocious ability to climb'. The family bonded together, supported each other, and held their glossy, well-kept heads high.

Although the Sandhurst passing-out ceremony seemed a positive sign for the future of the four-year relationship, it suffered a setback a few weeks later when Kate's family invited William to come and stay with them for New Year. The Middletons had booked Jordanstone House set in snowy countryside on the outskirts of Alyth, North of Dundee. William had originally intended to come, but then changed his mind, which upset Kate. They hadn't seen each other over the festive season, as William always spent Christmas with the Queen and the rest of his family at Sandringham. Although certain things were changing with the times within the royal family, Christmas at Sandringham was still strictly a royal affair. It meant they would not be able to spend Christmas Day together unless they were married.

Unfortunately, the trend of their spending time apart continued into the new year. The day before Kate's twenty-fifth birthday, William left to join his first regiment, The Blues and Royals, stationed with the Household Cavalry at Bovington Barracks in Dorset. He would be away for much of the following months, and the three-hour drive meant that he wouldn't necessarily be returning to London every weekend.

In 2007, many had been predicting a royal wedding, and Woolworths were already stocking wedding paraphernalia. Just before Kate's birthday, Diana's former private secretary Patrick Jephson wrote a feature for the *Spectator* called 'The Next People's Princess' about how she would be a glamorous and much-needed addition to the royal family. When Kate went to work on the morning of her birthday, she was swarmed with more aggressive paparazzi than ever before.

Interest in Kate had now crossed over into harassment, and the following day, William requested that his press secretary release a statement, reading, 'He wants more than anything for it to stop. Miss Middleton should, like any other private individual, be able to go about her everyday business without this kind of intrusion. The situation is proving unbearable for all those concerned.'

The following month, William gave Kate a pre-Valentine's present of a green enamel Van Cleef & Arpels diamond-framed makeup compact, featuring a polo player about to hit a pearl. Gestures were one thing, but the couple weren't spending any time together and cracks were beginning to show, and then to deepen.

William was stationed outside London and they spent significant amounts of time apart over the next few months. They were also still young, and both figuring out what they wanted from life, but Kate felt like she had less of a say in their relationship and their future. Although she had her job at Jigsaw, she wasn't sure it was what she wanted to do long-term. William had to fulfil his duties – that was his destiny – but where did that leave her? She wasn't sure herself which direction she would like to take – should she use her art history degree and go into a related field, should she pursue her interest in fashion or should she maximize her past experience and family contacts and go into the party industry like her parents? Or would all of it be moot? If they ended up getting married, she would be required to submerge herself fully in royal life, and this would take some time and preparation.

Additionally, William didn't seem to be in any rush to head back to London at weekends. His quarters in his barracks were small, like those of the other men, fitted with just a single bed and not conducive to a couple staying for the weekend. So if they wanted to see each other, it would mean his making the effort to go to London or Berkshire. He started spending a lot of time with the rest of his barracks, going out drinking and dancing.

Then when he did make it back to London, on one occasion, he went out clubbing to Boujis with friends and flirted with another girl, which was in the papers the next day. Kate grew increasingly fed up, and felt his behaviour was disrespectful.

They attended the Cheltenham Festival together, but whereas the previous year it seemed that Kate could do no wrong as she hung out in the royal box with Charles and Camilla, this year she and William looked unhappy and out of sorts. Their matching decades-older tweed outfits were indicative of the rot that had set into their relationship. A few days later, William was back in his barracks and went out to nearby Elements nightclub in Bournemouth. The normally cautious prince was drunk and enjoying himself, surrounded by glamorous half-naked girls. In one picture he appeared to be holding the breast of Brazilian Ana Ferreira. Another clubber on the same night, Lisa Agar, said William was flirty – dancing and making suggestive comments. The pictures and quotes were in the papers the next day, and Kate and William were both embarrassed. However, there was no disguising the fact that William was unsure of their future together. When Charles was in a relationship with Diana and it reached a crossroads, Prince Philip said to him that he needed to take action one way or another and Charles proposed. When William was faced with a similar dilemma he went the other way.

CHAPTER EIGHT

The Sizzler Sisters

The last time Kate and William went out together before they split was with their friends Hugh and Rose van Cutsem, whose wedding they had attended two years earlier. On 31 March 2007, the foursome had a quiet night out in the van Cutsems' local the King's Head pub in Bledington. By the time Kate flew to Ireland with her mum on 3 April, the relationship of four years was over. Kate was devastated, but instead of just weeping at home in a darkened room, she got busy. Nothing gives a problem some perspective than getting away from it, and flying to another country was even better. Kate and Carole had gone to Ireland to support Carole's friend Gemma Billington, who was showing a private exhibition of her paintings. After viewing the exhibition, mother and daughter attended the champagne reception, and made the most of their visit by touring the National Gallery of Ireland.

William decided to celebrate the end of his relationship with a trip to Mahiki. The news of their split was not yet public, but those around him at the club were made aware when he leaped on to a table, shouting 'I'm free!', before slipping into his version of the robot dance, made famous by England footballer Peter Crouch, and suggesting to his friends that they drink the menu.

The following day the news of their split broke, but it wasn't long before William was having second thoughts. Mindful, perhaps, of the decision his father had made when he was in his twenties and let Camilla go, William did not want to make the same mistake. Kate, however, needed some convincing. He had broken her heart, and she wanted to make sure that if they did get back together it would be for the right reasons, and that she would be assured things would change. She signed up for a charity challenge with an all-female dragon boat racing crew called the Sisterhood, who billed themselves, A-Team style as, 'An elite group of female athletes, talented in many ways, toned to perfection with killer looks, on a mission to keep boldly going where no girl has gone before.'

William spent the summer at his barracks, and in his free time he fulfilled royal duties, played polo and enjoyed a few nights out with friends. Meanwhile, Kate said yes to a slew of invitations and in public was more sociable and vibrant than she had been for some time. She was soon joined in London by Pippa, who had just finished university and moved into the Chelsea flat with Kate. The two girls would have spray tans and blow-dries together, and decide which social events to attend. For some time, Kate had felt like she wanted to edge towards a more stable and mature lifestyle, favouring chilled nights at home and family events. However, she was still only twenty-five, and was now a single girl with the world at her feet – and a taxi waiting outside.

Although she was heartbroken, she wasn't going to show it. For her breakup diary, her dresses were shorter, her tops lower and her outfits racier. There were numerous nights out to hotspots where she had been a regular with William, and her swirl of brunette hair and carefully folded bronzed limbs as she entered and exited taxis was a common sight throughout April and May. She attended some diverse events. She and Pippa were at luxury jeweller Asprey for the launch of *Young Stalin* – a biography written by Tara Palmer-Tomkinson's brother-in-law Simon Sebag Montefiore. Kate also went to a party to promote the film *Rabbit Fever*, which was about women obsessed with the infamous vibrators. A world away from the frumpy ageing tweeds of two months ago, Kate wore a slinky off-the-shoulder top and silky skirt with a bare midriff, caramel tan and sun-kissed hair. Inside the party she wore pink silk bunny ears, danced and 'teased all the boys'.

Although Kate embarked on a breakup social whirl, inside she was in pain. Training with the Sisterhood helped distract her and also make her feel better. The twenty-one girls involved were aiming to row across the channel to raise money for the Ben Hollioake Fund, who raise money for the CHASE Hospice Care for Children, and another children's hospice charity, Babes in Arms. Kate got involved through her old school friend Alicia Fox-Pitt, and fellow rower Emma Sayle recalls, 'Kate was very down and I think the training became her therapy. Kate had always put William first and she said this was a chance to do something for herself.'

The team trained on the Thames in the leafy London borough of Chiswick from 6.30 a.m., and Kate threw herself into training. She very quickly proved herself. 'It wasn't a question of, "Oh, she's Kate Middleton so she makes the team,"' Emma told the *Daily Telegraph*. 'She has had to prove herself. We launched the challenge in November and Kate joined in April. Our coach said she could only join if she was up to it.' Thanks to years of sporting training, and an ongoing regime of tennis and swimming, Kate was more than up to the task. In her engagement interview, she said of the breakup, 'I think at the time I wasn't very happy about it, but actually it made me a stronger person, you find out things about yourself that maybe you hadn't realized. I think you can get quite consumed by a relationship when you're younger ... I really valued that time for me as well, although I didn't think it at the time!'

She was still licking her wounds when she headed to Ibiza for some sun and headspace with her brother James and friends, including Marlborough classmate Emilia d'Erlanger. Once more, they stayed at their Uncle Gary's villa, and it was noted by Gary's wife that Kate spent a lot of time on the phone.

Meanwhile, though William had wondered what other options he had out there, it turned out he'd had what he wanted all along. He and Kate secretly got back together on 9 June, when she attended a party at his barracks to celebrate the end of training. The theme was 'Freakin' naughty' and William wore hot pants, vest and policeman's helmet, while Kate was dressed as a naughty nurse. There were blow-up dolls hanging from the ceiling and sexy waitresses handing out lethal cocktails. Outside was a bouncy castle and plunge pool, but William and Kate stuck to the dance floor, and that night she stayed over at his barracks. William later said, 'We were both very young ... We were both finding ourselves and being different characters. It was very much trying to find our own way and we were growing up so it was just a bit of space and it worked out for the better.'

One month later, on 7 July 2007, Princes William and Harry stood on stage at Wembley in front of 63,000 people. Harry shouted out, 'Hello, Wembley!' and the crowds went crazy. The two princes had decided to honour the ten-year anniversary of their mother's death with an uplifting tribute concert on what would have been her forty-sixth birthday. It was a huge moment for the boys – not just personally, but in terms of moving further and more officially into the public arena as well. Slipping into their seats in the royal box, Harry sat next to his girlfriend Chelsy Davy, while William sat next to his best friend Thomas van Straubenzee. However, two rows back was Kate, accompanied by her brother James. After the princes had welcomed everyone, Elton John kicked off proceedings with a rendition of 'Your Song' – the song that William and Kate later chose for their first dance on their wedding day. The concert rocked to the sounds of Take That, Duran Duran and P Diddy, while cousins Princesses Beatrice and Eugenie, Peter and Zara Phillips, and Earl Spencer's daughters Kitty, Eliza and Katya all sang and danced. The evening was a huge success.

Afterwards, William and Harry were in a more relaxed informal mode. The eyes of the world weren't on them anymore, and they had pulled off this emotional and jubilant extravaganza. That night they both had the women they loved by their sides. Harry and Chelsy had been together for three years and had also had their ups and downs, but for William and Kate, they were done with breakups and makeups, this time they wanted to be together forever.

William and Harry had wanted to thank everyone involved with the concert properly for their involvement – and did so with an amazing party. Many people offered their services for free, and there were tropical fish swimming below a Perspex dance floor, oysters and raspberry vodka jellies being passed around, and dancers in cages. Kate had worn a respectable white Issa mac to the concert, but for the party she slipped it off to reveal a thigh-skimming white lace slip dress, and she danced with William to one of their favourite tracks, Bodyrockers' 'I Like The Way (You Move)' before finding a discreet corner lit by candles and scattered with rose petals to sip mojitos, kiss and whisper in each other's ears.

A few weeks later, they were together again for Camilla's sixtieth birthday party at Highgrove. It was a black-tie event, and Kate wore a long cream dress and sipped champagne as William mouthed the words of Frank Sinatra's classic 'It Had To Be You' to her. She had been smuggled in to avoid publicity, but once inside the pair were happily ensconced and enjoying the glow of this new honeymoon period.

Unfortunately, a downside to her reunion with William was that she needed to pull out of the race with the Sisterhood. She had wanted to complete the challenge, and William was behind her 100 per cent. However, as legal letters had previously been issued requesting her privacy, it would be seen as hypocritical if she then undertook the high-profile publicity-dependent endeavour.

Kate didn't attend the church memorial for Diana at the end of August as this was a more formal occasion for Diana's close friends, family and the people she had worked with. This year, 2007, became one where the late princess's presence was felt more than ever. Shortly after the concert and church service, the inquest into Diana and Dodi's deaths was reopened. The previous year, the findings of Lord Stevens, former commissioner of the Metropolitan Police was that, 'There was no conspiracy to murder any of the occupants of that car.' Dodi's father, Mohammed Al Fayed, however, remained unconvinced with the findings and so the case rumbled on. Although William and Harry had been living their lives and growing into well-rounded young men, it was hard for them to find any kind of peace and move on when the process scratched and scraped on for ten years.

Kate had been by William's side for half that time. It's perhaps one of the reasons she had ended up becoming so special to him, forging a profound bond that no one else could ever comprehend. A few days after the case was reopened, Kate and William were photographed leaving Boujis and were chased by the paparazzi. It was astoundingly poor behaviour and William, understandably, made a complaint. However, the couple also decided to make themselves less vulnerable to this kind of behaviour. After a few years of kicking up their heels at their favourite haunts, they began to do most of their socializing behind closed doors.

Kate and William had a lot to discuss, and some lost time to make up for. In September, they flew to the Seychelles – a string of far-flung islands in the Indian Ocean. They stayed in the Desroches Island Resort, checking in under the names 'Martin and Rosemary Middleton', and went kayaking and snorkelling in the shallow coral reef. At night they relaxed over a candlelit supper on the beach. It was during this break that they made an agreement with each other. For the next few years, they would work and enjoy their lives, knowing that at some point when the time was right, they would be husband and wife.

In the autumn, after spending one year with the company, Kate left her job at Jigsaw. She had enjoyed it, and was becoming increasingly interested in fashion, but ultimately it was not the career she wanted to pursue. She wanted to explore her love of art and photography, as well as get involved with more charity work. After spending time photographing stills for the Party Pieces website, she toyed with the idea of becoming a professional photographer, and threw herself into curating an exhibition at the Bluebird restaurant. Here, she arranged the work of photographer Alistair Morrison, whom she had known since her days at St Andrews after she asked his advice about a photography project she was working on as part of her degree. She had visited his studio in Windsor, and they had stayed in touch. The photographs were of A-list celebrities including Tom Cruise, Kate Winslet, Catherine Zeta-Jones and Sting, and were taken in special photo booths around the world, including in the Dorchester Hotel in London, as part of a project to raise money for the United Nations' children's fund, UNICEF. 'She is very, very good, and it shows.' Alistair told the *Daily Telegraph*. 'She takes very beautiful detailed photographs. She has a huge talent and a great eye. I'm sure she will go far.'

That autumn, Chelsy Davy was having problems with Harry. Kate and Chelsy were never a natural fit as friends, but they were in the same position and supported each other when it mattered. After Kate and William had split in the spring, Chelsy – who was studying in South Africa – sent texts to Kate, and now Kate was able to return the support. Chelsy had left her sun-drenched home in South Africa to study law at Leeds University, partly to be near Harry. However, the twenty-three-year-old prince was not showing his appreciation, and she was left feeling neglected. Kate spoke to her and advised her to give him some space, and sure enough it wasn't long before Harry and Chelsy were back together. Both royal girlfriends felt better after their respective times apart. They were able to gather themselves, and steer the relationship in a direction they were happier with.

Kate and William spent a lot of time together over the autumn and winter. She learned how to stalk deer on the Balmoral Estate, and in a stark contrast to the previous year they were by each other's sides throughout much of December. Kate accompanied William on a pheasant shoot in Windsor, where she helped collect the dead birds, they went ice-skating at Somerset House in London, and they even welcomed in the new year together, spending some time together on the Balmoral Estate.

In a pattern Kate was becoming used to, two days before her birthday, William left for the RAF training college in Cranwell, Lincolnshire, which was a little like Sandhurst and where he would start learning how to fly. He had his heart set on becoming a helicopter pilot and it would mean a lot more studying over the next few years. It was very hard work and there was no chance of drinking binges like before, as pilots can't drink alcohol for ten hours before they fly. He was living in halls of residence again, and the fifteen-feet square room with its single bed was not big enough for a couple to spend weekends together, so when Friday came, William would travel to Kate in London and they would spend their time at Clarence House. She would cook him dinner and they would watch DVDs. They were happy, close and in love, leading a very extraordinary, ordinary life. During the week, she was working for Party Pieces, and helped launch their new offshoot company First Birthdays, which focused mainly on baby celebrations. She spent her hours engrossed in sorting out the catalogue for the company and taking the photos.

For the third consecutive year, Kate attended the Cheltenham

Festival. However, in a marked contrast to the previous breakup year, this time she looked sharp and youthful in a short midnight-blue Ted Baker mac, knee boots and a black trilby, and was escorted by William's best friend Thomas van Straubenzee. She was happy and it showed.

Throughout her life, Kate had never been reliant on a boyfriend for happiness, and had always flourished when she was single. When she was in a relationship that felt unstable, she wasn't at her best, but now the air had been cleared and she felt secure. It was her time to flourish again.

CHAPTER NINE

A sapphire from Ceylon

P rinces in fairy stories have been known to ride up to their princess on a white charger as a declaration of their love. However, for this very modern prince, who preferred jeans and loafers over a suit of armour, and a smartphone over a lance, William decided a Chinook helicopter would do the job. Of course, it was also useful for his training, but there's no mistaking a grand gesture when one is being made. Once the operation had been cleared, he executed his landing in the field next to the Middletons' Berkshire home, where Kate was staying at the time. As Michael Middleton said in his father-of-the-bride speech at their wedding, 'I knew things were getting serious when I found a helicopter in my garden. I thought, "Gosh, he must like my daughter."' At the time it caused a huge furore because it was deemed an unnecessary manoeuvre and therefore a waste of taxpayers' money; however, the RAF had been using such test-runs for years and it was actually incorporated into his training as a practice exercise.

Kate was there on 20 April 2008 when he got his wings in Lincolnshire. And, in a sure sign that a more official role was sure to follow, she was filmed walking alongside William through the RAF base, after arriving with his aunt, Lady Sarah McCorquodale. And sure enough, just one month later came the moment that meant something very important indeed. It was time for Kate to meet the Queen.

When she attended the wedding of Peter Phillips and Autumn Kelly in May 2008, it was already going to be a significant occasion for Kate. She would be representing an absent William at the wedding of one of his own family members, but it also happened to be the first time she would be meeting his grandmother. William was out of the country, as he had previously received an invitation to his old friend Jecca Craig's wedding to Hugh Crossley in Kenya. But Kate was comfortable attending the royal wedding on her own. She already got on well with William's family, including Harry, and she spent a lot of time on the day with him and Chelsy. The Queen had wanted to meet Kate for a while and this was the perfect opportunity – everyone was relaxed and knew each other, and it was a happy day without the pressure of a formal one-to-one meeting. For the occasion, Kate wore a floaty black Issa dress with a sheer panel at the front, with a rose-pink fitted jacket and black-netted hat. And the Queen approached her – coming over for a chat.

The couple had decided to have their big day covered by *Hello!* magazine and afterwards were publicly criticized. The British royal family had always maintained they were not celebrities – they were focused on family and duty, and yet the wedding ran alongside interviews with Gisele Bündchen and *Holby City* star Tina Hobley. Buckingham Palace later admitted they had made an error of judgement, and when Peter's sister Zara got married four years later just two official photos were released to all of the press.

Another notable occasion where Kate was present in a formal, royal setting was at Windsor Castle in June, when William was inaugurated as a Royal Knight Companion of the Order of the Garter. The Order is the most senior and the oldest order of chivalry in the country, and is awarded by the Queen to those who have shown extreme loyalty or military merit. The knights meet every year at Windsor Castle, when new members are inaugurated, and after a meeting and lunch they process down to St George's Chapel for a church service, returning to the castle in open-topped carriages. William felt privileged and proud to be part of it, although also slightly embarrassed in his requisite ostrich-feather plumed hat and floor-length cloak. Kate watched the procession standing next to Harry, who roared with laughter at his brother, while Kate suppressed giggles and looked on proudly.

That summer, Kate also started taking on some charity work, alongside working for the family business. In June, she once more donned a stunning floor-length creation for the second Boodles Boxing Ball. This time it was a fuchsia gown by Issa, who had swiftly become one of her favourite designers. She was at the charity ball to support the couple's friend, James Meade, who was fighting under the name 'The Badger', as well as Jecca Craig's husband Hugh 'The Hitman' Crossley.

While she was there, Kate made a new charity connection with the Starlight Children's Foundation, which was set up by former *Dynasty* actress Emma Samms. Starlight aims to grant wishes to seriously ill children, and entertain them in hospitals and hospices, and that night the charity was the beneficiary of the event. It was also attended by Bianca Nicholas, who has cystic fibrosis, and at the age of fifteen had her wish granted by Starlight when she recorded an album. Three years later, Bianca had another wish granted when she sang live at the ball in front of nearly 1,000 people, including Kate, who was there with William and Harry. 'She was singing from the boxing ring and she was such a tiny person that the top of her head barely cleared the top of the boxing ropes', recalls Starlight's Chief Executive Neil Swan. 'Everybody was just amazed by this young ladies' fantastically powerful voice.'

As Bianca exited the boxing ring, William got up and invited her to come and join them at their table, so she spent most of the rest of the evening sitting chatting with him and Kate. 'They made her feel like she was the most important person on the table,' says Neil. 'She came back with her jaw on the floor, saying, "They were asking me all these questions!" She was completely bowled over by the fact they genuinely took such an interest in what she was trying to do – about how she was getting on with her singing and how the cystic fibrosis affects it.' Bianca now works for Starlight herself and keeps a picture of her with Kate, William and Harry above her desk. 'So you can tell from that how important it was to her,' says Neil. It was important to Kate as well, as she kept in touch with the organization and used her connections with her parent's company to work on a project over the next few months.

Every December, in the run-up to Christmas, Starlight throw around 220 parties in children's hospital wards and hospices around the country, providing them with party packs that contain tableware and goody bags, as well as presents, entertainers, food and drinks. 'It becomes quite a major operation for us, because we're dealing with thousands of children,' explains Neil. 'It became Kate's project to help us put together party packs, and it was very much Kate who initiated it. We had a need and she very kindly provided a solution for us. The actual design of pieces and the thought process of how about doing it this way or that way – that was very much down to her. This was very much her project.' The goody bags themselves were interactive items that the children could colour in, and contained colouring pencils, an activity pad, box of stampers a Beanie Baby and panpipes, while the party-wear was all colour-themed to co-ordinate with Starlight's signature colours.

As well as working on the Starlight Christmas party project, in September 2008, along with sister Pippa and their friend Holly Branson, Kate attended the Day-Glo Midnight Roller Disco. It was held in aid of two charities – Place2Be, the youth counselling service, which, after her marriage, would become one of her patronages, and Tom's Ward at Oxford Children's Hospital, which had been set up in memory of fellow Marlborough pupil Tom Waley-Cohen. He died after suffering ten years' with bone cancer, and his brother Sam, who went to St Andrews with Kate and William, got Kate involved with the event. On the night, Tom's parents skated and Kate skated. She wore yellow hot pants and a green sequined top – and fell over, for which she was criticized for a lack of dignity by some of the media, but nevertheless, the event raised £100,000.

William had spent a year at Sandhurst, a year in the army, four months with the RAF and two months with the navy. In the autumn it was announced to much surprise that he was not going to become a full-time royal, as many had anticipated. He was going to train to be a search-and-rescue pilot for eighteen months, which could then lead to a post for three years if he was successful. William explained that, after training in the military for nearly three years, he would have very much liked to have gone to the front line and fought for his country, as Harry had done the previous year in Afghanistan. However, because William was second in line to the throne, it would be too much of a security risk. He would be targeted by the enemy and it would not only distract from the job he was trying to do, but would also put him and his men at further risk. Since he could not fulfil his wish of going to the front line, he decided that he would instead like to serve the people of Britain in a different way.

It was a different step for someone who was becoming a senior member of the royal family. Princess Anne made the full-time move into royal duties when she was eighteen; Charles had been twenty-eight by the time he had been to university and completed his military training. This decision meant that William would be at least thirty-one when he became a full-time royal. But it was necessary for him to have this time, and the Queen was supportive. He would have a lifetime of obligation and duty, so a few of years in his twenties doing something that was personally fulfilling and useful made no difference in the overall scheme of things. It also meant that Kate had some time to get used to her position, rather than rushing into royal duties when she was still very young.

As usual, she and William spent Christmas apart. He had his duties at Sandringham and she was in Mustique with her family. The Caribbean island had become a favourite with the Middletons thanks to its old-fashioned charm – and the fact that it is totally private. While other Caribbean destinations had been modernized, Mustique was still the exclusive and luxurious destination that had been a favourite of Princess Margaret and Mick Jagger. Even when they were on holiday, the Middletons remained active and spent their time horse-riding, playing tennis and practising yoga.

Kate always returned from her holidays as brown as a berry, and as soon as she was back, she headed up to the Scottish Highlands to welcome in the New Year with William at Birkhall, the Prince of Wales's Scottish residence. This was the first time William and Kate had spent the New Year at Birkhall while Charles and Camilla were there as well. They went shooting and had family meals at the end of the day at which Camilla would make Kate cry with laughter. A lot of time had passed since Camilla and William's first meeting, and not only did he get on well with his stepmother, but so did Kate.

In another change from previous years, William was around for Kate's birthday. Two days later, he started at the Defence Helicopter Flying School at RAF Shawbury near Shrewsbury. It meant they were apart during the week, but they would usually spend their weekends together. Kate divided her time between her flat in London and her parents' home, where she still slept in her old bedroom. In London, the couple would usually stay at Clarence House, or William would head down to Bucklebury to spend some time with Kate and her family.

The Boujis and Mahiki nights were a thing of the past and they chose to spend time with a few close-knit friends, at dinners, drinks parties and weekends of country pursuits. Kate and William's friends have been a constant and impenetrable support to them both, and for the most part are people who would not be recognized in photos, or even by their names alone, such is the private nature of their friendships.

Kate was still close with many of her Marlborough girls, such as Alicia Fox-Pitt, who was now a guide for adventure travel company Wild Frontiers, and was there for Kate with the Sisterhood during Kate's breakup with William. Emilia d'Erlanger is an interior designer who runs her own business called d'Erlanger and Sloan. She is an old friend of Kate's from Marlborough who also went to St Andrews, and was another confidante who helped Kate through the breakup. The Sloan part of the company is Anna Sloan – another St Andrews contemporary with whom William had been to stay in Nashville. Emilia later married David Jardine Paterson, the brother of Pippa Middleton's ex, JJ Jardine Paterson. Kate was also still good friends with other Marlborough girls Trini Foyle, Hannah Gillingham and Alice St John Webster, as well as her own ex, Willem Marx, with whom she still socialized. Kate also had a handful of new friends including society girl Astrid Harbord, Virgin heiress Holly Branson, and Sophie Carter, whom she met through mutual friends. She and William also remained in touch with former university pals Olivia Bleasdale, Oli Baker, Ollie Chadwick-Healy, Sam Waley-Cohen and Rupert Finch – who married one of William's old friends, Lady Natasha Rufus Isaacs.

There were others who had started out as William's friends, but who – along with their partners – became Kate's friends too. From birth, William had been extremely close with the four van Cutsem brothers, Edward, Hugh, Nicholas and William, who on paper sound like characters from a Jilly Cooper novel – all tall dark and handsome, with a penchant for country pursuits. Their father, Hugh, went to Cambridge with Prince Charles and so their sons had grown up together. Major Nicholas van Cutsem was the Life Guard who later took command of the mounted soldiers at Kate and William's wedding, while William was an usher when Nicholas married Alice Hadden-Paton. Edward van Cutsem is Charles's godson and was pageboy at his wedding to Diana. Harry and William were both ushers at Edward's wedding to Lady Tamara Grosvenor and, like William, Edward is involved with work at the Craigs Lewa Wildlife Conservancy in Kenya. The younger Hugh van Cutsem and Lady Rose Astor are the parents of Grace van Cutsem who was bridesmaid at William and Kate's wedding and who covered her ears to block out the sound of the fly-past on the balcony. William was also an usher at their wedding. Meanwhile, William van Cutsem later married Prince William's ex, Rosanna Ruck Keene.

Other good friends include event-rider Harry Meade who was at Eton with William and is married to primary school teacher Rosie Bradford. The first time Kate and William arrived at a wedding together was to theirs, which was shortly after Kate and William's engagement but before it was made public. Guy Pelly and Arthur Landon were the perennial singletons in the group. Arthur is one of Britain's richest young men, with a fortune estimated at up to £500 million. He is a film-maker and former model and child star, and later accompanied Prince Harry on his fateful trip to Las Vegas. Guy has owned a string of top London clubs including the upscale tequila bar Tonteria, where William and Harry attended the stag do of Thomas van Straubenzee.

Known as 'Van', Thomas is perhaps William's closest friend. His Uncle Willie was a friend of Diana's, and the boys had known each other since childhood. They went to Ludgrove and Eton together, and Thomas became engaged to Lady Melissa Percy, whose brother George was Pippa Middleton's flatmate in

Edinburgh. It was Thomas's younger brother, Henry, who was killed in a car accident when William was at St Andrews, and William and Harry both became patrons of the charity that was set up in his memory. It was also Thomas who escorted Kate to the Cheltenham races the year after her breakup with William, and sat next to William at the Diana concert. He had also accompanied them on assorted holidays and. alongside Prince Harry, gave a speech at Kate and William's wedding.

Kate had truly been welcomed into the royal fold. She had represented William at family events, accompanied him to formal occasions, including his passing out at Sandhurst and Garter Ceremony, and she had holidayed with Charles and Camilla. She was a seemingly impeccable companion for William, but the summer of 2009 she was thrown a curveball by none other than her uncle, who had unwittingly been involved in an elaborate press sting.

On 19 July, the country woke to some lurid headlines in Sunday tabloid the *News of the World*, relating to Kate's uncle, Gary Goldsmith. Kate had been made aware the story was going to run the day before, but there was nothing that could be done about it. Splashed across newsstands was the headline, 'I called Wills a f***er!' and inside were several pages alleging that Gary had offered to supply their reporter with cocaine as well as the number of a woman who could provide call girls.

Gary was the victim of the paper's famous 'fake sheik' Mazher Mahmood, who had previously set up Sophie, Countess of Wessex, and later Sarah, Duchess of York. At his Ibiza home, Gary recounted to the undercover reporter how William and Kate had been to visit and how, while playing a game, William had broken some of his ornamental glass pyramids, which had prompted the expletive-ridden headline. However, it was not only the allegations that were concerning, but the fact that Gary was so open and unguarded about his niece and her boyfriend with someone whom he had only just met – reporter or not. If he was saying these things to one man, it would seem to indicate that he was as indiscreet with countless others. However, the Middletons and the royal family appreciated that everyone makes mistakes and that perhaps it is not about the mistakes someone makes, but about how they deal with them that is important. Gary has always been the wild one in the family but Carole adores her little brother, and Kate and her siblings have always been very fond of their uncle.

'The very first phone call I got was from Carole, on behalf of the family,' Gary told *Hello!* magazine. 'She just apologized and said this wouldn't have happened if it wasn't for the fact of who Kate was dating.' He also explained that they had laughed about the broken glass pyramids when they met at a later date, and that William had blamed it on James Middleton who was also there. Prince Charles called Kate to reassure her there was nothing to worry about, and William was very protective of his girlfriend and her family. For William, it was another reason to dislike the press even more. He was more angry with them than he was with Gary. Meanwhile, Gary felt bad for what had happened and flew home to London to lie low. He kept his head down and three years later was invited to the royal wedding.

That year, Kate had also continued her work with Starlight on a children's art project which culminated in an exhibition and fundraising gala. She had recently joined the small committee for the Maggie & Rose children's club, which had been co-founded by her friend Rose Astor. Camilla, Duchess of Cornwall's daughter Laura Parker-Bowles was also a committee member.

They invited many children – both well and unwell – to attend workshops spread over the course of the spring and summer, and held at the Maggie & Rose venue. Each workshop was attended by a different artist – some already established, others up and coming – and the children were encouraged to create their own works in the style of each artist. They had approached Starlight to get involved with their project.

On 28 September, the children's artwork was displayed in London's Saatchi Gallery, and during the day there were large tents pitched out in front of the gallery, where children were invited to come along and participate in more artwork. Starlight Chief Executive Neil Swan explains, 'As a member of the committee, Kate was in one of the tents. What was really nice, was that there were kids and their parents going in and out of the various tents all day and participating in all the different activities that were going on, and I don't think anyone realized that in one particular tent, Kate was in there doing it. She was just doing her thing, helping to entertain and encourage the children. It was ultra low-key and she was just getting on and mucking in as one of the team.'

Then, in the evening, it was all-change for Kate into a gun-metal grey plunging floor-length Issa gown for the fund-raising gala. Guests were invited to come along and view the art during a champagne reception, and there were various artistic auction pieces also on display, including a Vivienne Westwood customized rocking chair. As a Maggie & Rose committee member, Kate hosted a table, which included her mother Carole who bid £8,000 for a ski holiday. Then, as everyone took their seat, William slipped in and sat next to Kate. This was her night and he was there to support her.

In turn, Kate was involved with a Henry van Straubenzee

memorial evening in December. William and Harry had become patrons of a charity set up by his parents to raise funds to help improve the quality of education in Ugandan schools, and on the night of the event, Kate helped decorate the venue beforehand and clear up afterwards.

At the beginning of 2010, Kate celebrated her twenty-eighth birthday with William and her family in Bucklebury, and just days later there was cause for celebration once more as William completed his advanced helicopter training course. Kate was there by his side when he graduated. Shortly afterwards, William moved to Anglesey to start an eight-month course at RAF Valley, which would teach him to fly the Sea King helicopters that they use in rescues. The couple went skiing in Courchevel, France, with the Middletons and raced round the resort on snowmobiles. William was heard calling Michael 'Dad' and he and Kate held hands under the table.

When they returned, Kate too started spending a lot more time in Anglesey, and they found a lifestyle there that suited them both. The island of Anglesey is situated on the Northern tip of Wales, and is joined to the mainland by two suspension bridges. It is also home to the famous town with the longest name in Britain: Llanfairpwllgwyngyllgogerychwyrndrobwllllantysiliogogogoch, which roughly translated means, 'The Church of St Mary in a hollow of white hazel near a rapid whirlpool and near St Tysilio's church by the red cave'. Remote and beautiful, Anglesey is made up of a great deal of coastline, providing wide panoramic views of the Irish sea. Inland has vast fields of big woolly sheep, tangled hedgerows, ancient trees, stone walls and crumbling old buildings grown over with ivy. William had been there before with his father when he was twenty-one, when he and Charles went to a local food fair and William had flipped burgers. William had also done some training there as part of his work experience programme in 2005, and it had struck a chord with him.

Similarly to St Andrews, Angelsey was windswept and wild. It was also a rather well-kept secret – very romantic with long sandy beaches, and uncluttered views of the sky. Kate had always been a fan of the great outdoors, so they were able to spend their time making the most of their surroundings. Once again, they got used to the sounds of seagulls, but whereas St Andrews had the student community and a buzzing social scene, Anglesey was even more remote, with patchy mobile phone coverage, and homes often a car-drive apart. Surprisingly, however, there is also a recording studio on Anglesey, and so as well as getting used to the sight of royalty in the local supermarket and pubs, locals would also occasionally spot members of One Direction and The Wanted in their sleepy rural surroundings.

Kate and William rented a whitewashed five-bedroom farmhouse on the Bodorgan Estate for £750 a month, from Sir George and Lady Meyrick. It meant they were living on private property, with their protection officers based in the house's converted outbuildings, they were surrounded by dense woodland, and the only access was by private road, which was ideal for them. The farmhouse was also situated right beside the beach. The estate had deer-stalking, fishing and game shooting and they enjoyed making the most of all that was on offer, as well as hearty walks and Sunday roasts with the Meyricks.

William worked shifts on a rota with his co-workers, which would include his doing eight twenty-four-hour shifts a month. He was stationed at his base while he was on duty, much like a fireman in a fire station, ready to scramble if a call for help came through. The search-and-rescue team were basically the fourth emergency service, dealing with sea and coast-related accidents. They could be called upon to rescue a capsized boat, a walker who was lost or fallen, oil rig workers, those in a remote community cut off by floods or anyone lost at sea. He was in a team of four and when the call came they could be in air in fifteen minutes in the daytime or forty-five minutes at night.

Over the next couple of years while they were based there, Kate looked after everything relating to their home. Unlike other royals before him, William employed no domestic staff, and Kate took care of it all. She shopped in their local Waitrose, Tesco and Morrisons, but also favoured local produce. She had always been known as a fantastic cook, and she now started honing her skills and experimenting with new dishes. She would visit the local butcher to buy liver so that she could make pie gravy, or a chicken for William's favourite roast dinner, and she also started making her own sausages. She was also a fan of Mary Berry's cookbooks and enjoyed baking sweet treats, including William's favourite chocolate brownies, and cakes for him and his co-workers, which one of them reported were 'pretty good'. She also stocked up on jam jars from the local hardware store for her homemade strawberry and plum preserves, which were later a Christmas present for the Queen.

At home together in the evenings the couple enjoyed watching *The X Factor* and *Downton Abbey*, and worked their way through a box set of *The Killing* after it had been recommended by Camilla. They played scrabble, and went for walks on their local beach. They also explored the island and neighbouring area, travelling on William's motorbike, which gave them complete anonymity. One of their favourite spots was the White Eagle pub just down the road in Rhoscolyn, which had a reputation as one of the best pubs on the island. It was quiet, with a log fire, and mix and match tables and chairs. While William would opt for home-made burgers and chips with a pint of bitter, Kate preferred fish or salad with white wine or sparkling water. They also popped into the Seacroft at Trearddur Bay, and on the other side of the island in Beaumaris, they ate meals in Ye Olde Bulls Head. They would also go to the cinema at Llandudno Junction.

William tended to go out on his own more than Kate, as he had his co-workers to socialize with, but when Pippa came to visit the two sisters went walking on the beach at Llanddwyn Island, and Kate also went to an antiques fair at the Mona Showground where she haggled over the price of a pair of nineteenth-century Japanese Imari vases from £180 down to £160. When William successfully completed his training in September 2010, it was a cause for massive celebration. Kate had been patiently supporting him for the past three years as she quietly worked and made the most of her non-royal status, but they both knew what was coming and knew that, although many good things would follow, it would also mean a life of increasing duty and less time to themselves.

He and Kate had spoken of marriage and they knew it was on the cards, but it hadn't been the right time … until now. They both knew that they had found a good match in each other. They had tried to be apart and it didn't work. They knew they wanted to spend the rest of their lives together. 'We went through a few stumbling blocks as every relationship does,' he explained in their engagement interview. 'But we picked ourselves up and carried on and from where you have the odd problem where you're first getting to know each other, those have all gone and it's really being with each other and it's really fun.'

Buoyed by these feelings, but also touched by nerves, William decided that the time had come when they took a holiday together the following month. He wanted it to be special for Kate and one of the most beautiful places he had ever been to was in Kenya. He had always loved Africa – he felt anonymous there, and that no one really cared about his status. He had first visited in 1998, with Harry and their family friends the van Cutsems, and they had met the Craig family. Elephants and black rhinos had been decimated by poachers and the Craigs had turned their entire 61,000 acre reserve over to house a rhino sanctuary, now called the Lewa Wildlife Conservancy. William had returned to Kenya for part of his gap year, staying with and working for the Craigs, and that is when he became involved with Tusk Trust, a charity that aimed to preserve the wildlife and educate the people in the local area about conservation. He had taken Kate back there after university and she had loved it too. Africa had had a profound effect on him from the first time he stepped foot on the country's red soil, and it was here that he wanted to propose.

When they first flew in, the couple stayed with the Craigs at Lewa Downs for the first part of the trip, spending some time driving round the estate watching elephants and rhinos. Kate and William then travelled on to the next part of their trip alone, with William – unbeknown to Kate – carrying his mother's priceless engagement ring in his backpack. They drove to the Rutundu Lodge, overlooking Lake Rutundu – two simple wooden cottages nestled in the Mount Kenya range, which was incredibly remote and had a stunning view of snowy peaks and forests of heather. At that time of year the scenery was more like the Scottish Highlands, and the evenings were cool so they enjoyed log fires and candles.

The lodge is self-catering and the couple arrived with a box of supplies. They went fishing for rainbow trout on the lake from the back of a rickety boat, but didn't catch any. That night, after William cooked dinner, they had each other, a log fire, cups of tea and paraffin hurricane lamps for company. Guests were told to stay inside after darkness fell, in case any stray wild animal was roaming around, but when inside was so inviting there was no need to leave. The wooden floors were warmed and softened with rugs, and they shared a wooden four-poster bed. In the morning, having been woken by a weaver bird tapping on the window, they rose early. William made breakfast and they went on another short fishing trip before their 10 a.m. checkout.

At some point during their stay, they travelled further up to Lake Alice. This lake sits in an extinct volcano and is perfectly silent. It is surrounded by the lush green hills and the snowy peak of Mount Kenya, with small volcanic rocks bobbing on the surface of the turquoise lake. It is thought that it was here, in total privacy, surrounded by nature, that William proposed.

The ring he slipped on her finger was perhaps the most famous ring in the world. A slim eighteen-carat band of white gold, set with a twelve-carat oval Ceylon sapphire, surrounded by fourteen diamonds. Back in 1981, after Charles had proposed, Diana was sent a selection of rings to choose from by the royal jeweller, Garrard of Mayfair, and she selected the sapphire piece that at the time cost £28,500.

After Kate had accepted William's proposal, the couple headed back to Lewa. It had been Kate's first time to that part of Africa, and in the visitors' book she wrote, 'Thank you for such a wonderful 24 hours! Sadly no fish to be found, but we had great fun trying. I love the warm fires and candle lights – so romantic! Hope to be back again soon. Catherine Middleton.'

The newly engaged couple kept their secret to themselves for a while and flew back to the UK to spend some time in

Scotland before they started breaking the news to their friends and family. William spoke to Michael Middleton first, to ask for his permission, but when Kate first saw her mother, she wasn't sure what she had been told. 'We had quite an awkward situation because I knew, and I knew William had asked my father, but I didn't know my mother knew ...' Kate recalled in the engagement interview. 'My mother didn't make it clear to me whether she knew or not, so both of us were there sort of looking at each other and feeling quite awkward about it!' When William told Harry, he was thrilled and told him, 'I have a sister.'

The news had not been made public yet, although it was noted when they attended the wedding of William's friend Harry Meade that, unusually for the couple, they arrived together. They were all set to make the announcement until on 2 November came the sad news that Kate's grandfather Peter Middleton had died. He had been her last surviving grandparent. Kate dealt with her grief and helped support her father and the rest of her family, as they spent some time together and attended Peter's funeral on 12 November. They were then able to move on to the more joyful news of their public announcement.

On 16 November 2010, the Buckingham Palace Twitter feed announced, 'The Queen and the Duke of Edinburgh are absolutely delighted at the news of Prince William and Catherine Middleton's engagement.' The press were gathered at St James's Palace, which is the most senior royal palace in the UK. For the announcement, Kate selected the instantly iconic midnight blue silk jersey Issa dress, and a delicate lapis and diamond necklace from Tiffany. She and William also recorded an interview with Tom Bradby – ITV's political correspondent who had filmed some of William's gap year and a documentary with Harry to raise awareness of life in Lesotho, Africa.

For most of the public – and the press – it was first time they had heard Kate speak, or been able to watch the way she behaved, and observe what she and William were like together. 'Kate was very nervous – very, very nervous – understandably,' Bradby told Penny Junor for her book *Prince William: Born to be King*. 'She knew that everyone was curious, no one had ever heard her speak and they were probably going to make up their minds for the rest of their lives what they thought about her in the next twenty minutes.'

She needn't have worried. Although her nerves were noticeable, she came across as warm, genuine and good-natured, and the couple's chemistry was obvious, as they laughed and joked together. 'That day was really special,' recalls *Sunday Express* royal correspondent Camilla Tominey. 'We just thought it was gonig to be a photo shoot and possibly a Q&A, we had no idea we were going to have tea with the couple. One minute we were working out what to ask, and the next I had a cup of tea in my hand, talking to Kate.' Conversation quickly moved to the very famous piece of jewellery Kate was now wearing. 'When I first met her, the first thing I noticed was the ring,' Camilla continues. 'I thought it might be the Princess of Wales's but I wasn't sure so I pointed to it and said, "That looks like a family heirloom." She replied, "Yes, it was William's mother's, so it's very special." It was such an understated way of saying it, you could have knocked me down with a feather.'

The couple went back to nearby Clarence House for a drink to celebrate and relax – the relief of the public side of the announcement over. For eight years, Kate had been observed and scrutinized and, at worst, followed, harassed and derided, but the engagement changed everything. Because Kate had been seen as a low-key figure who had only bit by bit increased in significance in William's formal life, she had rather flown under the public radar until this point. When she stepped out in her midnight-blue silk and bouncy blow dry with the ring on her finger and faced a wall of photographers' flashbulbs, she became one of the most famous women in the world.

She was immediately given round-the-clock security, and her own police protection officers. She was used to William's security people being around and they were for the most part an unobtrusive presence. They wore tailored suits to fit into their surroundings, with a gun in a holster in the small of their back. All of the royal family's protection officers had a police background, and once an officer was selected they undertook extensive courses where they mastered advanced driving, first aid, physical fitness and firearms proficiency. If they passed, then they would go through the national bodyguard course, where they were also taught the importance of personal skills – the people they would be guarding had to trust them, so they would need to be able to build a good rapport. Kate was assigned a team of three – Detective Sergeant Ieuan Jones, who was formerly one of Prince Harry's protection squad, and a pair of female officers – Inspector Karen Llewellyn, who previously ran the team protecting Princesses Beatrice and Eugenie, and Sergeant Emma Probert – who were soon dubbed Cagney and Lacey.

William's private office also organized a series of private meetings at which Kate met with senior members of the royal household, key advisors to William and Harry and representatives from some of William's charities so that she could learn about the work she would be undertaking.

William went back to work, while Kate stayed on and off with her parents over the next few months as she planned the wedding with the help of sister Pippa. Over the past two years, Pippa had worked for event planners Table Talk, and also recently for the more specialist wedding planners Blue Strawberry, so was the perfect planning companion for the bride to be. In fact, if there was a time for the ethos of the Middleton family business to swing into action, this was it. Their whole livelihood and the drive behind it was about celebrating and making the most of an occasion, so with them in a key role the event was sure to include many personal touches.

A pair of engagement photos were also released to mark the event – taken by Peruvian superstar snapper Mario Testino. The couple posed in St James's Palace in complementing outfits, while soothing music played to help them relax. Testino was already known for his stunning portraits of William's mother Diana, as well as Kate Moss and Angelina Jolie, and William had also chosen him to take his official portraits to commemorate his twenty-first birthday.

The new shots of William and Kate were for the history books. Kate's style choices also helped earn her the tag of 'the High Street Duchess'. For the more formal image, William opted for a navy suit, white shirt and tie, while Kate wore a cream dress from Reiss. When it came to the more relaxed image of them cuddling, William selected a light brown jumper over an open-necked white shirt, while Kate chose a cream blouse from Whistles – and with both outfits she wore white topaz 'hope egg' earrings from Links of London.

The couple were apart for Christmas, as William was on duty, but once January had arrived it was full steam ahead – the wedding was just four months away. The date they had decided on – 29 April 2011 – was on a Friday, which the government declared would be a public holiday. The whole country was looking forward to the occasion almost as much as the couple themselves. William was presented with a list of hundreds of people who he should invite to the wedding and felt his heart sink. The occasion would be 100 per cent formal, with no room for their personal guest list or special touches. He spoke to the Queen and she told him to tear up the list, invite his friends and start from there.

As time rolled on, speculation fizzed about the choice of designer for the wedding dress, which was being made under the most top secret of circumstances. There was already endless speculation in the press as to what it would look like, but if the designer was known beforehand, there was the real possibility that someone might guess almost exactly what it would look like and run a design in the papers, which William would see. This was to be a traditional wedding and Kate wanted to be able to surprise her groom.

In February, she and Pippa went for a girls' lunch with Camilla and her daughter Laura at Koffmann's restaurant in top London hotel the Berkeley. The lunch lasted three hours, and Kate finished her meal with the restaurant's famous pistachio souffle. The group were all laughing and joking and talking at the same time, and the waiters found it hard to get a word in edgeways. At one point, Kate joked about the wedding buffet and said they could have pizza, while Camilla suggested that sausages on sticks were always good.

At the end of February, William and Kate undertook their first official engagement together. Most royal engagements can be broken down into three key areas: representing the country, charity work, and maintaining royal traditions. These official engagements are incredibly important – they get the family out among the people, and because of the colourful photographs that usually accompany the story, they draw attention to whatever it is that they are doing that day. Even in her mid-eighties the Queen is taking on a huge number of engagements, which often totals over 400 a year, while Prince Charles regularly clocks up 500–600. Royal offices are inundated every year with all manner of proposals, and each one has to be assessed, and either rejected or accepted very carefully. Now that Kate was officially going to be one of the family, a handful of engagements were drawn up for her to undertake alongside William before their wedding.

For their first official engagement together, William and Kate launched a lifeboat in their home-place of Anglesey. Already showing signs that she would make diplomatic gestures as part of her fashion choices, Kate's fascinator bore the insignia of the Royal Welch Fusiliers. Chris Jackson, who works for top picture agency Getty Images and has been photographing the royal family for the past ten years, recalls: 'I remember vividly the moment Kate stepped from the car onto the tarmac at Angelsey. Her poise and confidence were evident. Gone was the slight nervousness we saw on the announcement of the engagement. She had obviously spent the previous weeks receiving advice and training on how best to handle these occasions.'

The following day she and William returned to their old university of St Andrews to launch its 600th anniversary charity appeal. They stood in the quad outside St Salvators, which had been the scene of Kate's first year foam fight for which she wore bunches and loo roll. This time, eight years later, she was dressed in a scarlet Luisa Spagnoli skirt suit and the Princess of Wales's engagement ring.

In March, Kate and William completed their list of visits,

which made up the countries of the United Kingdom – after a low-key reception for the Teenage Cancer Trust in Norfolk, England, Anglesey in Wales and St Andrews in Scotland, they headed to Belfast in Northern Ireland for Shrove Tuesday, where they flipped pancakes.

Since Kate wasn't from an aristocratic family she didn't have a coat of arms. This needed to be rectified, as she would need one for official purposes. It was designed by the College of Arms in blue, red and gold, and featured acorns to represent the oaks populating her home county of Berkshire. There were specifically three acorns, representing the three Middleton children; the gold chevron in the middle signifying Carole's maiden name of Goldsmith; with narrow white lines on either side that resemble peaks, to denote the family's love of the mountains in the Lake District and of skiing. The brand-new coat of arms would be reproduced on the back of the wedding's Order of Service, along with William's on the front.

A discreet hen-do was thrown at a friend's house, organized by Holly Branson, and attended by a few handfuls of friends, including Rose Astor, Alice Haddon Paton, Olivia Bleasdale, Alicia Fox-Pitt and Astrid Harbord. Lastly, before the wedding, Kate was confirmed into the Church of England. When she eventually became queen, she would be married to the head of the Church of England, so she needed to be confirmed. The Bishop of London, Richard Chartres, was a friend of the royal family since he went to Cambridge with Prince Charles, and he conducted the low-key ceremony, which was held at the Chapel Royal in St James's Palace, and attended by just William and her family.

The next time she stood in a church it would be in front of three billion people.

CHAPTER TEN

'Just a quiet family wedding ...'

P rincess Anne and Captain Mark Phillips had been together only fifteen months when they got married. For Prince Andrew and Sarah Ferguson it was twelve months, while for Prince Charles and Lady Diana Spencer it was just nine. These royal weddings had all been whirlwind affairs, which all, sadly, ended in divorce, so when it came to Prince Edward, he and girlfriend Sophie Rhys-Jones learned from the past and spent six years together before they got married. Kate and William followed suit, and by the time they took their wedding vows they had been together for over eight years. They had been through breakups, bereavements, scrutiny, criticism and scandal. Their relationship had not only survived, but thrived – from the low-key beginnings in university digs, to a full-blown declaration of love thousands of miles away in the mountains of Africa. And on 29 April 2011, their big day had arrived.

The 29 April is the feast day of St Catherine, and the day of the month was also William's parents' wedding day – they had married thirty years earlier on 29 July. By entering into the royal family, Kate had sealed her fate and would eventually become the sixth Queen Catherine. Catherine of Valois had married Henry V, Catherine of Aragon, Catherine Howard and Catherine Parr were all married to Henry VIII, and Catherine of Braganza was married to Charles II. William would eventually be the fifth King William. For the time being, however, Kate and William had enough new titles to be getting on with. On the morning of the wedding, the Queen bestowed upon them the titles of the Duke and Duchess of Cambridge (when they are in England and Wales), the Earl and Countess of Strathearn (when they are in Scotland), and Baron and Baroness Carrickfergus (when they are in Northern Ireland).

Their wedding was understandably the cause of huge celebration, pomp and tradition. It involved Westminster Abbey, the Archbishop of Canterbury, royalty from all around the world and three billion people watching. However, times had truly changed since the days of the Queen's own children getting married. In her autobiography, Sarah, Duchess of York wrote of her wedding breakfast, 'It was lavish and proper and dull, that lunch.' Adding, 'All the pomp had been fine, but I wanted to be a regular bride – I wanted Andrew's best man to get up and make a funny speech ...'

Instead, Kate and William's wedding was to tread the fine line between a cause for countrywide celebration as befitting the second-in-line to the throne, but also a personal day for the happy couple and their families, which reflected a royal family that was moving with the times. Instead of riding to the Abbey in a carriage, Kate and William both opted for cars. They also prepared their own wedding prayer, in which they asked God to, 'keep our eyes fixed on what is real and important in life' and to 'help us serve and comfort those who suffer'. Instead of the more formal sit-down wedding breakfast at Buckingham Palace, there was a buffet, and the guest list got smaller and less formal as the day went on, so that it would end with dinner and dancing in the evening for just their close family and friends.

Well-wishers had flown into London from all around the world, and started lining the streets around the Abbey and Clarence House three days beforehand. By the eve of the wedding, the streets had the feel of a music festival, with lines of tents up and down the pavements that at some points pooled into whole encampments. People wore tiaras and cardboard Kate and William masks. There was a King Charles spaniel in a veil. Some revellers were up early eating scotch eggs and drinking wine out of plastic glasses, others bore flasks of tea and bundled up against the April showers in Union flags and fleeces, while some erected picnic tables and drank champagne. One woman wore the same peach-coloured wedding ensemble complete with feathered hat and white gloves for days on end as she waved for the cameras and was interviewed by TV crews. *Big Issue* sellers handed out Quality Street chocolates, taxi drivers crawled past with their windows wound down taking pictures on their camera phones, and helicopters whirred overhead.

The Middletons travelled up from Berkshire having booked out the entire seventy-one rooms in the Goring Hotel for three nights. The hotel was the Queen Mother's – and is still the Queen's – favourite London hotel, and it is still owned by the Goring family, who founded it a hundred years ago. It is situated close to Buckingham Palace, and has the timeless elegance of bygone era. While many top London hotels strive for a contemporary relaxed feel, the Goring still revels in feeling grand and formal. When Carole, Michael, Pippa and James arrived two days before the wedding, they did so in a lightning storm of flashbulbs. The countdown had begun. Kate arrived at the hotel the following day in her own explosion of camera flashes, and stayed there for the night before her wedding.

The speculation as to the designer of Kate's dress had been building to fever pitch, and when a figure bundled in a huge parka with the hood up, stepped out of a car with just a ballet pump on display, it was all the papers had to go on. *Who did the ballet pump belong too?* Meanwhile, William and his best man, Prince Harry, spent the night before in Clarence House with their father and Camilla. As darkness fell, William had an idea to go with Harry out into the crowds to meet some of the people who had been camping out. It was a very modern gesture by a member of the royal family, and very typical of William. He asked one of the campers, 'Have you got a Jacuzzi in there?' While Harry invited himself into another camper's tent. After dinner Harry went on to the Goring and stayed up drinking in the bar with Pippa, on-off girlfriend Chelsy and some of their friends. When he decided it was time to leave, around 3 a.m., he clambered up on to the balcony, jumped off into a flowerbed and loped back to nearby Clarence House.

Although William was a little more sensible that night, he still didn't get much sleep, later recalling, '[The crowds] were singing and cheering all night long, so the excitement of that, the nervousness of me and everyone singing – I slept for about half an hour.'

On the morning of the wedding, William had breakfast with Harry and James Middleton at Clarence House as, by 8.15 a.m. the 2,000 guests started arriving at the Abbey. Westminster Abbey was once a Benedictine Monastery and a total of thirty-eight coronations have been held there since William the Conqueror was crowned there in 1066. Kate and William's wedding would be the sixteenth royal wedding to be held there. The first was that of King Henry 1 on 11 November 1100. While the Queen was still just a princess, she married Philip Mountbatten there in 1947. It was also the venue for Diana's funeral in 1997.

When Kate and William were deciding on a venue, they were able to consider several possibilities, including St Paul's Cathedral, where his parents had married. However, the abbey was a good choice for the couple, as it was like a church within a church – making it seem like the event was more private than it actually was. Their family and closest friends would sit in the Quire area, where the majority of the ceremony would take place, and most of the rest of the congregation would sit in the nave and two transepts. The abbey also had a shorter processional route back to Buckingham Palace than St Paul's, which meant it was cheaper and easier to police – an important consideration in a time of recession. It was Kate's idea to bring England's green and pleasant land inside the abbey, and so guests were greeted by the incredible sight of an aisle lined with towering maple trees and hornbeams in full-leaf, while corners and ledges were leafy with azaleas, rhododendrons, potted beeches, wisterias and lilacs.

Kate had chosen the 'language of flowers' as the theme for her wedding décor, using the Victorian practice of florography, where each flower had a meaning. Of the seventeen different types of flowers iced onto the wedding cake, she diplomatically selected English rose, Scottish thistle, Welsh daffodil and Irish shamrock – as well as sweet william for her husband, bridal roses for happiness, acorns for strength and lily of the valley for sweetness and humility. The theme was also carried through in the design of her dress, while the abbey was scented with her favourite Jo Malone orange blossom candles. The floral designer was Shane Connolly, who had worked on Charles's wedding to Camilla, and his displays in the abbey were left up for a week after the wedding so that visitors could see them, before they were given to charities or sent to Charles's home, Highgrove, for re-planting.

Celebrity guests included David and Victoria Beckham (as president of the Football Association, William had come to know David after working on the failed 2018 World Cup bid, and they had remained friends), Elton John, Guy Ritchie (who they became close to through their mutual friend Guy Pelly), Ben Fogle (he and William were both involved in adventure travel for charity), Rowan Atkinson, Joss Stone, plus swimmer Ian Thorpe, and from the world of rugby, Gareth Thomas and Clive Woodward (William is patron of the English School's Swimming Association and the Welsh Rugby Union).

Also on the guest-list were Diana's brother Earl Spencer and his daughters; Harry's on-off girlfriend Chelsy Davy; family friend Tara Palmer-Tomkinson; forty members of overseas royalty; political leaders David Cameron, Nick Clegg and Ed Miliband; and London mayor Boris Johnson. US president Barack Obama was not invited as, since William was not yet heir to the throne, but second-in-line, it was not a state occasion, and so there was no obligation to invite any heads of state.

The abbey did contain a large number of personal friends,

including two of William's exes – Arabella Musgrave and Olivia Hunt, and two of Kate's – Willem Marx and Rupert Finch. Echoing Dorothy Goldsmith's funeral, when many villagers were invited, locals from the Middletons' home of Bucklebury were there, including the landlord of the Old Boot Inn, the postman, the shopkeeper and the butcher, along with several people whom the family knew from their holidays in Mustique, including the island's tennis coach, yoga teacher and equestrian centre manager, as well as Basil Charles, the owner of Mustique's famous Basil's Bar. There were also representatives from William's charity affiliations, including a girl who had been a rough sleeper who had been helped by William's charity Centrepoint. He had met her on one occasion, remembered her, and sent her an invitation.

William was driven to the service with Harry in a claret Bentley. He had served with the army, navy and air force and could have chosen any of their uniforms but wore the iconic scarlet tunic of the Irish Guards, which along with the bright blue sash, white gloves and gold sword slings were all made by Kashket & Partners, with sweat-pads sewn in, so there would be no unsightly marks on the day. In February, the Queen had given him the honorary rank of Colonel of the First Battalion of the Irish Guards, which was his most senior title in any of the armed forces, and she told him to wear their uniform for his wedding. Harry wore the uniform of a captain of the Household Cavalry, and exchanged words with his mother's family, the Spencers, while William chatted to the Middletons as the brothers moved up the aisle. Carole was accompanied by her son James, and wore a sky-blue wool crepe coat-dress by Catherine Walker and matching hat by Jane Corbett.

There is a strict protocol about who arrives when within the royal family, and after the dignitaries and other guests had arrived, it was their turn. They mostly rolled up in silver minibuses. Cousins Peter and Zara Phillips arrived with their partners, Autumn Phillips and Mike Tindall, their mother Princess Anne, and her husband Timothy Lawrence. They were followed by the Earl and Countess of Wessex, and the Duke of York with his daughters Princesses Beatrice and Eugenie, who themselves were followed by Charles and Camilla in a burgundy Rolls-Royce. Charles wore a Royal Navy No. 1 ceremonial dress with blue sash, and Camilla wore a champagne silk dress and blue and champagne coat by Anna Valentine, with a Philip Treacy hat.

Finally, the Queen and Duke of Edinburgh arrived, also in a burgundy Rolls-Royce. The Queen wore a primrose-yellow Angela Kelly dress and matching hat, with her diamond True Lover's Knot brooch. As his grandmother took her seat, William was in the side chapel with Harry, collecting himself. Outside, the Coldstream Guards played show tunes and singalong numbers along the route, and keepsake souvenir programmes were sold by military cadets and cub scouts so the crowds could sing along with the hymns.

Finally, the moment had arrived and, as Kate emerged from the Goring at 10.51 a.m. in a mist of veil, the crowds roared. She had kept herself calm and collected while she was getting ready, and wanted as few people around her as possible. Apart from her immediate family, there was just the dress designer to help with the final touches, her hairstylist and a Bobbi Brown makeup artist who stuck to Kate's brief to make her look as natural as she always did, while Kate added her own eyeliner and a spritz of White Gardenia Petals by Illuminum.

The designer of the dress was revealed to be Sarah Burton, who had taken over Alexander McQueen's design house after he had died two months earlier. Sarah and Kate had dreamed up a creation that was reminiscent of Grace Kelly's wedding dress when she married Prince Rainier of Monaco, but with Kate's choice of hair and makeup, she still looked contemporary. Made from ivory satin, the skirt of the dress was designed to echo the silhouette of an opening flower, and was lightly traced with individual flowers cut from hand-stitched lace, blooming into a nine-foot train at the back. The lace cut-outs included roses, thistles, daffodils and shamrocks to represent all four countries of the United Kingdom, and the nipped-in corset was sheathed in ivory lace, which had been handmade by the Royal School of Needlework at Hampton Court Palace. The ivory duchesse satin shoes were also Alexander McQueen. Before working on the dress, the seamstresses had to sign confidentiality agreements and it is said that when working on it they had to wash their hands every thirty minutes to keep the lace pristine.

The veil was made from ivory silk tulle with a trim of hand-embroidered flowers, and held in place with the Cartier halo tiara on loan from the Queen. The tiara had been made in 1936 and belonged to the Queen Mother – a gift from her husband King George VI. Kate had told her hairstylist, James Pryce, that she wanted to look like herself on her wedding day, she wanted William to recognize her and she wanted to be natural. James spent weeks practising the up-do with a £6.50 tiara from Claire's Accessories, explaining later in an interview with the *Sunday Times*, 'We came up with a unique concept for securing it. We backcombed the top to create a foundation for the tiara to sit around, then we did a tiny plait in the middle and sewed it on. I've never seen anything like it in my life.'

The only other pieces of jewellery she wore apart from her ring and tiara were a pair of diamond earrings by Robinson Pelham, which had been designed for her and were a gift from her parents. They were made up of diamond-set oak leaves and acorns in a tribute to the oaks of her home county, and of England, and were hung with pear-shaped diamonds. Kate carried a shield-shaped bouquet of lily of the valley, sweet william and hyacinth. And, like every royal bride since Queen Victoria, her bouquet also contained a sprig of myrtle cut from a bush grown from the sprig of myrtle in Queen Victoria's own wedding bouquet.

Michael helped Kate fold her dress into the claret Rolls-Royce Phantom VI in which they made the nine-minute journey to the abbey. They were followed by Kate's wedding party. Her sister Pippa was maid of honour, and also wore a memorable floor-length white Sarah Burton creation, and the four little bridesmaids and two page boys were all drawn from William's family and friends. The bridesmaids were Grace van Cutsem (William's god-daughter), Eliza Lopes (Camilla's granddaughter), Margarita Armstrong Jones (the queen's great-niece) and Lady Louise Windsor (Prince Edward's daughter). They all wore ivory ballerina dresses with pale gold silk sashes and ivory pumps with Swarovski crystal buckles, and the smallest ones were kept in line by Pippa. The two pageboys were both William's god sons – William Lowther-Pinkerton (the son of William's private secretary) and Tom Pettifer (the son of former nanny Tiggy), and they wore red and gold military style outfits designed by Kashket & Partners.

The Very Reverend Dr John Hall, Dean of Westminster, was to

conduct the service; the Archbishop of Canterbury, Dr Rowan Williams, head of the Church of England, officiated; and the Bishop of London, the Right Reverend Richard Chartres, as confidante to the royal family, who had confirmed both William and Kate, delivered the address.

As Kate and Michael were greeted by the Dean of Westminster, Sarah Burton made sure the dress fell correctly. Michael later said he wasn't nervous because he had Kate on his arm, and even told friends it felt like a dream until he opened the newspaper the following day. As she and her father walked down the aisle, the choirs of Westminster Abbey and Her Majesty's Chapel Royal, St James Palace, sang Charles Hubert Hasting Parry's 'I Was Glad'. Harry looked back as Kate started walking down the aisle, and reported back to his brother 'Right, she is here now ... well, she looks beautiful, I can tell you that.' At the top of the aisle, the couple set eyes on each other, and William murmured to Kate, 'You look beautiful,' before joking to Michael, 'Just a quiet family wedding ...'

The first hymn, 'Guide Me, O Thou Great Redeemer' was the last hymn to be sung at Diana's funeral, and so as well as making sure his mother would be a part of the day by giving Kate her engagement ring, she was also there in many other ways. The Dean of Westminster then greeted the couple and conducted the service, before the Archbishop of Canterbury stepped in for the exchanging of vows.

Starlight Chief Executive Neil Swan had been invited to the wedding, along with other staff members, and recalls, 'I think one of the loveliest moments was when Kate and William were taking their vows. Inside the abbey there was absolute silence and a total air of solemnity as they said, "I do", but of course it was being broadcast live to the crowds, and we heard this huge roar from outside. At that moment everyone's faces inside the abbey cracked into huge smiles.'

Kate's wedding band – according to royal tradition – was made from a nugget of Welsh gold already owned by the royal family from the Clogau St David's mine. It was a slim gold band made by Welsh jewellery family Wartski, but in another break from tradition William chose not to wear a wedding ring. James Middleton then gave the lesson Romans 12. It was a proud moment for Kate's younger brother as he has dyslexia and chose to memorize his words rather than risk reading it and getting muddled. 'I had to re-type the whole thing phonetically,' James explained to the press later. 'And that's how I learned it. In that way I became confident in it and then I felt like I was perfectly capable of doing it. At the end of the day, whether it was in a little church or Westminster Abbey didn't matter, it was me, as a brother doing a reading for my sister and her husband at their wedding, and I wanted to do it right.'

Then the Bishop of London delivered the address, musing, 'In a sense, every wedding is a royal wedding with the bride and the groom as the king and the queen of creation, making a new life together so that life can flow through them into the future.' After the rousing hymn 'Jerusalem', the couple moved to the shrine of Edward the Confessor for the signing of the marriage register with their witnesses Charles, Camilla, Carole and Michael.

The choir sang Parry's 'Blest Pair of Sirens' before Kate and William made their way back down the aisle, with Kate stopping to curtsey to the Queen, who smiled. They were followed out of the abbey by Harry and Pippa, and the rest of their families. As they did, seven trumpeters sounded out a new fanfare composed specially for the wedding – 'Valiant and Brave' – which is the motto used by RAF 22 squadron with whom William was serving as a search and rescue pilot. Outside the abbey, the peal of bells and the rolling cheers of the crowd were joined all over London by boats on the Thames blasting their horns, and Big Ben sounded as other churches pealed all over the city.

At 12.15, the couple started their journey to Buckingham Palace in the 1902 State Landau, which had been built for Edward VII for his coronation. Charles also used it to travel to his wedding thirty years earlier, returning in it with Diana. Posies and a horseshoe were left for Kate on the seat – a gift from staff at the royal mews. William stepped in first, taking Kate's bouquet as she settled in next to him with her dress billowing like a cloud at their feet. As they processed through the streets, they passed war memorials, where William saluted and Kate respectfully bowed her head. His charity Centrepoint arranged for the release of thousands of balloons, and the crowds cheered and cheered. The couple were escorted by officers of the Life Guards with their blonde horsehair plumes, and officers of the Blues and Royals of the Household Cavalry mounted regiment, commanded by their friend Nicholas van Cutsem. The Queen and Philip followed behind, and then came two carriages of bridesmaids and pages along with Harry and Pippa. Then the final carriage contained the Middletons with Charles and Camilla.

They were all welcomed into the quadrangle of Buckingham Palace by the Welsh Guards military band, before heading upstairs for the official portraits taken by Hugo Burnand, who had been the wedding photographer for Charles and Camilla. At this stage there was a secret appearance from an extra guest to keep the little bridesmaids entertained. 'Harry pulled this wiggly worm out of his pocket in the carriage to keep them amused!' Camilla later revealed. 'Eliza loved it so much that she wouldn't let go and it even made the official photographs. Can you believe it? She was holding on to my finger but in her other hand was this worm.'

The wedding-day balcony appearance has become royal tradition, but it was only at Charles and Diana's wedding that a kiss became a part of it. An ecstatic and overwhelmed Kate and William obliged the crowds with not one but two kisses, as their families beamed and three-year-old bridesmaid Grace van Cutsem covered her ears to protect them from the roar of the crowds, and then from the ceremonial fly-past.

The Queen hosted the formal part of the reception for 650 guests, which broke with tradition and was in the form of a buffet. The couple chose a lot of organic food from the UK, and 10,000 canapés were created by royal chef Mark Flanagan and battalion of twenty-one other chefs. The fancier canapés included Cornish crab salad on lemon blini, pressed duck terrine with fruit chutney, and smoked Scottish salmon rose on beetroot blini. However for those with simpler tastes there was also cheese straws, fishcakes and glazed chipolatas. Back when they had their girls' lunch and Camilla suggested sausages on sticks, Kate was listening.

Sweet canapés included rhubarb crème brûlée tartlets, milk chocolate praline with nuts and raspberry financiers. The couple and the guests sipped Sir Winston Churchill's favourite tipple Pol Roger champagne, and Kent-produced Chapel Down wines, while Charles's official harpist Claire Jones played as guests mingled through nineteen state rooms. It was at this reception that the couple cut their official wedding cake, which was actually made up of twelve separate cakes for the base and another seven individual cakes for a total of eight tiers.

Above: Holding her father's hand while looking radiantly happy on her wedding day, 29 April 2011.

Below: Stepping out of the 1902 State Landau as the newly married couple arrive at Buckingham Palace.

Above: In July 2011 Kate and William visited Canada and North America on their first foreign tour as a married couple.

Left: In Calgary, Kate hugs six-year-old cancer sufferer Diamond Marshall.

Above: Evidently having fun watching a rodeo demonstration in Calgary …

Below: … and creating art while on a visit to Inner-City Arts in Los Angeles.

Above: The three young royals wave to the crowds from the royal barge during the Diamond Jubilee Pageant on the Thames, 3 June 2012.

Right: With the couple's cocker spaniel puppy, Lupo, at the Tusk Trust Charity Polo Match, June 2012.

Above: Very much at ease, Kate accompanied the Queen to a children's sports event at Vernon Park during a Diamond Jubilee visit to Nottingham.

Below: Celebrating the Men's Team Sprint Track Cycling Gold medal at the London 2012 Olympic Games.

Kate and William headed East representing the Queen overseas as part of her Diamond Jubilee celebrations. They started out in Singapore (*above*) before going on to the South Pacific island of Tuvalu (*below*).

Left: Kate, seen here on an Art Room visit to Rose Hill Primary School in Oxford, is passionate about supporting young people through her patronages and charitable work.

Below: After treatment for a rare and extreme form of morning sickness, Kate and her relieved husband leave the King Edward VII Hospital on 6 December 2012.

The mother-to-be was positively blooming at a Garden Party in the grounds of Buckingham Palace in May 2013.

At 3 p.m. they thrilled the crowds with another modern touch, as William drove Kate to Clarence House in a blue Aston Martin BD6 which had been his father's twenty-first birthday present from the Queen. For the occasion, the number plate was JU5T WED, and it was decorated with red and blue ribbons and an L plate. In all the excitement, William forgot to take the handbrake off, but all sounds were drowned out anyway by a huge Sea King helicopter flying overhead which had been organized as a surprise by the RAF, and dipped in salute to the couple. Once back at Clarence House, they changed into fluffy dressing gowns to relax and watch the coverage on TV, while the Middletons entertained their guests at the Goring, and the Queen and Prince Philip headed to Windsor, as they wanted the rest of the day to be for the younger members of the family and the couple's friends.

The evening reception at Buckingham Palace was thrown by Prince Charles, and as guests started drifting in at 7 p.m., they were piped through the candle-lit courtyard by bagpipers and welcomed with flutes of pink champagne and Bellinis. Everyone had changed into black tie, and Kate had selected a floor-length white satin Sarah Burton gown, with a diamante-encrusted waistband, and fluffy white angora bolero. Dinner was served at 8.30 p.m. and had been prepared by Anton Mosimann. It included seafood from Wales, lamb from Highgrove and an assiette of desserts followed by tea, coffee and petit fours, before Harry gave his much-anticipated speech. He paid tribute to Kate, who he had previously referred to as his sister, saying, 'I've got to know Kate pretty well, but now that she's becoming part of the family, I'm really looking forward to getting her under my wing – or she'll be taking me under her wing probably. She's a fantastic girl. She really is. My brother's very lucky, and she's very lucky to have my brother. I think the two of them are a perfect match.'

Kate had managed to hold it together all day, but had tears in her eyes during the speeches. Harry also regaled guests with stories of being beaten up by his brother, and teased him about his romantic style and receding hairline. He also said how proud their mother would have been, and told the guests, 'William didn't have a romantic bone in his body before he met Kate, so I knew it was serious when William suddenly started cooing down the phone at her.' After Michael took his turn, speaking warmly of William, his new son-in-law returned the gesture in his speech, and was followed by his friends Thomas van Straubenzee and James Meade. After Kate and William had cut the their second wedding cake – a nursery favourite of William's made from bashed-up Rich Tea biscuits and lots of melted chocolate, Harry announced, 'We have a little surprise,' and led guests through to the Throne Room, which had been transformed into a nightclub with mirror balls, sofas and cocktails.

Ellie Goulding then performed Elton John's 'Your Song' for their first dance, followed by her own hit 'Starry Eyed' when the bride and groom were joined on the dance floor by Charles and Camilla. Ellie performed for two hours and ended with 'She Loves You' by the Beatles, which segued into a raucous disco fuelled by Crack Baby cocktails, mojitos and sambuca shooters, while Harry danced on windowsills and stage-dived off them. He and Chelsy were the life of the party, and William and Kate were dancing to 'The One That I Want' from *Grease* among their guests. For those who danced themselves up a whole new appetite there were vans dispensing bacon sandwiches and ice creams outside in the quadrangle, which is usually where recipients of OBEs and MBEs pose for pictures, while inside the palace were popcorn machines and bowls of Haribo sweets.

At 2.30 a.m., everyone was ushered outside for a firework display in the courtyard and the couple then slipped off in a yellow Fiat, sticking their heads through the roof as they were driven round two corners to their suite at the palace. Guests were then ushered out into the night and many went back to the Goring Hotel, including Harry with Chelsy, Beatrice and Eugenie – they travelled in coaches, Harry still clutching his microphone, while other guests piggyback raced down the road. Kate and William spent their first night of married life in the Belgian Suite in Buckingham Palace, and as they slept, newspaper presses were not only churning out millions of front-page balcony kisses, but many column inches inside were dedicated to a brand new star ...

CHAPTER ELEVEN

Her Royal Hotness

When Pippa Middleton stepped out of the Goring on the morning of the 30 April, she stepped out into a world where everyone now knew her name. Just two days earlier, she was 'Kate Middleton's sister', now her name was on everyone's lips and it was a case of, 'Who's that girl?', swiftly followed by, 'Does she have representation?'

Unlike the breakout star of a film, or a band with a must-have album, she hadn't done anything to achieve this fame, she had simply stooped to adjust the train of her sister's wedding dress. In doing so, her dress hugged her curves, and by the end of the day three Facebook pages had been created in honour of her derrière, and Justin Bieber was tweeting his approval. In the weeks and months that followed, Pippa was dubbed 'her royal hotness', while cosmetic surgeons offered the 'Pippa butt job' for $20,000, and US adult entertainment company Vivid were offering $5 million for her to make an x-rated movie.

However, look again and what people saw was actually very little of anything. While some had described her dress as 'tighter than a coat of paint', it was – although slinky – actually a perfectly respectable gown, eminently suitable for the occasion. It was the idea of what lay beneath, the suggestion of a curve, that drove people into a frenzy. And it didn't hurt that she was pretty, and young, and seemed to get on very well with Prince Harry …

But who was this girl who had captured people's imaginations? Born Philippa Charlotte Middleton on 6 September 1983, she is just twenty months younger than her sister and was soon nicknamed Pippa. When the family returned from Jordan, she was just two years old, and while Kate headed off to school, Pippa attended the local nursery. She then followed her big sister to St Andrew's school where she too thrived. She was sporty like Kate and also got involved with drama and singing, joining the choir and the flute group the Tootie-Flooties. Afterwards at Marlborough College, she swam for the school and was captain of the hockey team. So far, so Kate, although their Uncle Gary believes the girls are quite different, stating in *Hello!* magazine, 'Kate works really hard at everything. She is brilliant at whatever she turns her hand to, but works at it, throwing herself into everything. Whereas Pip, everything seems to come very easily.'

It was after they finished at Marlborough that they started to follow different paths. When Kate was at St Andrews University, Pippa started at Edinburgh University. The fact that both sisters opted for Scottish universities may well have had something to do with their formative school years at St Andrew's school where they learned about Scottish customs and celebrations. In her book, *Celebrate*, Pippa declared, 'I have come to treasure

Scotland, a land cloaked in nostalgia and history, as one of my favourite places … there is something about the Scottish countryside that feels wild and romantic.' For many years it was Pippa who carried the haggis into her local pub the Old Boot Inn on Burns night, accompanied by bagpipes.

She and Kate had always been incredibly close, and because Edinburgh was only an hour by direct train from St Andrews, even when Pippa had moved hundreds of miles away from home, she still had her big sister close at hand. Not that she needed it. Pippa has always been vivacious and was more extroverted than Kate. At Edinburgh she studied English literature, and although Kate mixed with a lot of students who were public-school-educated, apart from a certain prince not many of her gang had titles. It just so happened that Pippa's did, and soon her group were dubbed 'the castle crew'. At weekends they took off to each other's family home in the country for shooting and fishing trips, or headed down to London to someone's family townhouse to make the most of the nightlife and attend dinner parties. Carole and Michael had bought a flat in Chelsea so both Pippa and Kate had a base there when they needed somewhere in the capital to stay. When it came to shooting, in a traditionally male environment where the women either followed behind collecting stray birds or met up with the party for lunch afterwards, Pippa got stuck in herself, and was good at it – on one occasion shooting twenty-three birds in one day. She also skied and played hockey.

As befitting her sporty nature, she didn't smoke or take drugs, and nor did she drink much, but she was lively, confident, smart and fun. People wanted her at their events and she had the boys falling at her feet. Like her sister, she was already something of a culinary whizz, and while other students were ordering takeout or living on microwave meals, Pippa was experimenting with making sushi. She would often visit Kate in St Andrews and accompanied her sister to the annual May Ball and assorted other balls.

Kate and the rest of the family also got to know Pippa's friends. One of them from Edinburgh was Thierry Kelaart, who became so close to the Middletons that in 2012, it was Michael Middleton who gave her away at her wedding. In Pippa's second year at Edinburgh she lived with Earl George Percy (whose parents own Alnwick Castle, which was used as Hogwarts in the Harry Potter films), and Lord Edward Innes Kerr (whose father owns Floors Castle, which was used as Tarzan's home in the film *Greystoke*). There were rumours that she dated George Percy but the pair were just friends. She actually went out with Jonathan 'JJ' Jardine Paterson, an Old Etonian who was from the Hong Kong banking dynasty. They were together three and a half years before splitting in 2007, which was the year Pippa left university and moved to London into the Chelsea flat with Kate.

Pippa moved to the capital in the crazy summer after Kate and William had broken up. The camera lenses of the world were trained on the LK Bennett-heeled suburb of Chelsea, and the girls were a photogenic treat. Sporting café-au-lait tans, luscious brunette locks, plenty of eyeliner and statement midi-dresses, by the end of the summer they had been dubbed 'the sizzler sisters'. Kate was back with William, while Pippa was enjoying her single status and working on her career. Like Kate, she was also employed by her parents company, but later got a job working for the event-planners Table Talk. As an event planner, she needed a good head for business as well as creative flair and a way with people, as the role involved researching and

planning the logistics of a big event, having the creative
to pull it off, and the charm to deal effectively with big-money
clients. She later also worked at their sister company Blue
Strawberry, with more of a wedding focus.

The year after she moved to London, things really started
happening for Pippa, and while *Tatler* had previously dubbed
her one of the 'wisteria sisters' this year they named her the
hottest singleton of the year. She had a bolder and more daring
style than her older sister – favouring stronger prints, brighter
colours, more detailing and a touch more cleavage. She started
editing *Party Times* – the online magazine that features on her
parents' website, and dated first Billy More Nisbett, a Scottish
socialite whose mother had been a lady-in-waiting to Princess
Anne, followed by diamond heir Simon Youngman. Because
she wasn't going out with royalty, she wasn't as scrutinized as
her sister, and she wasn't instantly recognizable to the public
or the press, so was able to attend many of the most glamorous
parties in London, as well as many sporting events of the season
including the races, polo and Wimbledon.

Her parents paid for her £11,000 membership for the
Queen's Club where she would play tennis with Kate, she would
also use the gym at Clarence House with her sister, and went to
Pilates at her small local studio Pilates On The Go. And so she
enjoyed her London life as a girl about town. She had a job that
was glamorous and fun, a handsome man on her arm, holidays
to Mustique, and a close and supportive relationship with her
sister. She had all the fun of her position with very little of the
negative attention that her sister was receiving. For now.

With many of her boxes ticked, as she entered 2009, she
decided to do more with her sporting prowess, and took up
tobogganing on the Cresta Run in St Moritz. Later in the

year she was briefly linked to Alexander Spencer-Churchill – a descendent of Sir Winston Churchill – but it was 6 foot 3 inches banker Alex Loudon who had soon caught her eye. Alex went to Eton with Prince William and was president of the college's elite-within-the-elite society Pop – their small group of prefects. He captained the under-15s and under-19s England cricket teams, but didn't make the transition to play professionally, instead going into the City. Like the other men Pippa had been linked to, he was tall, handsome, wealthy and good at everything, he was also welcomed into the family and was Pippa's guest at the royal wedding.

In the run-up to the wedding, Pippa was an invaluable help to her sister. Where most brides would have to ring around to compare prices, gauge numbers and discuss logistics, who better to help than someone who did all of that for a living.

After Pippa had done her duty on the big day, supporting her sister, holding the hands of the two smallest bridesmaids as they walked up the aisle and being escorted back down by Prince Harry, it was time for the evening event. The more formal part of the day was over, and she changed into a floor-length emerald-green silk Alexander McQueen gown, later heading back to the Goring Hotel with Harry, Chelsy, Beatrice, Eugenie and a gang of others. Sadly for the gossips, she was very much still with Alex at the time of the wedding and Harry spent the evening with Chelsy, so any wishful thinking about the siblings of the bride and groom starting any kind of romance was completely inaccurate. Pippa was actually quite friendly with Chelsy. Although Kate and Chelsy did get on, Pippa had more of a natural rapport with Chelsy than Kate did.

Despite the celebrations, the younger sister was Middleton-perfect the next day when she checked out of the hotel with her parents and brother. Immaculate in white jeans and blouse and a royal-blue jacket, she looked sharp and stylish, with no need to wear sunglasses to disguise party eyes.

That summer she continued working, and although she went through a brief split with Alex as he struggled to cope with her new found fame, they were soon back together, sealing it with a kiss at that year's Boodles Boxing Ball. She was once again incorrectly linked to her old university flatmate George Percy during the brief spilt, as they – along with other friends – enjoyed a city break to Madrid after the wedding. She was also working a few days a week for George's renewable-energy company, as well as a couple of days at Table Talk and a couple of days editing *Party Times*. The fact was, Pippa had lots of male friends. Although Kate had a number of male friends, she was closer to a strong clique of 'sisters', whereas Pippa had just a couple of girl friends and was often surrounded by men. She was often seen in public with one of her close male friends, which led to speculation that they were a couple. She was also good friends with banker Tom Kingston, but they too were just good friends who attended many sporting and social events together.

That summer, Pippa was the girl who everyone wanted on their party lists. A few years before, Kate had posed a conundrum where she was not royal, but close enough. Now she actually was royalty, with police protection officers, a press office and a voice, but Pippa had slipped into Kate's old role. Now Pippa was the one who wasn't royal but was close enough to it that she had to be careful. Again, she had no mouthpiece and no protection. It suddenly meant that she had to be a little more selective about which events she went to, and which business projects she undertook, so that she didn't create problems her sister.

Pippa started supporting more charity events, and threw

herself into more sporting challenges. The summer after the wedding she competed in the gruelling GE Blenheim Triathlon, and competed in the Highland Cross endurance race, running and cycling 50 miles in Scotland from coast to coast. The next year, in May 2012, she was to take part in the longest cross-country ski race in the world, the Vasaloppet Cross Country Ski Race in Sweden, along with her brother James. She and James were raising money for the Magic Breakfast charity, who provided a pre-school meal to inner-city children. Despite having never competed in cross-country skiing before, Pippa finished in the top third of over 15,000 competitors and impressed the organizers.

By this time she had split with Alex for good and was footloose and fancy free. In April 2012, she popped over to Paris to attend a lavish and riotous fancy-dress birthday extravaganza, thrown by French fashion entrepreneur Vicomte Arthur de Soultrait. The party featured dancing dwarves, burlesque strippers and half-naked girls sending sparks from their chastity belts with angle grinders. There was free-flowing champagne, and the host of the party posed on a throne wearing a dog lead. Pippa wore a Marie-Antoinette style mini-dress in fuchsia and gold satin, with a black leather jacket, and later smooched Parisian TV producer Antoine de Tavernost. The event provided some colourful newspaper copy, but she was simply a young single girl having fun and there was nothing wrong with that. However, the next day when she got a lift to the airport with the Vicomte's brother, he ended up brandishing a toy gun at the following paparazzi. This raised issues about whether his behaviour was irresponsible, and how Pippa needed to be careful about who she spent time with. There was no long-term solution. As Kate had found before her, Pippa would have to slowly find her own way, but the strong family support system, along with the Middletons' innate commonsense, would set her in good stead.

By the end of 2012, she had published her first book. The former English student wrote the home-entertaining bible herself, quitting her job at Table Talk to do so. *Celebrate* was a guide on how to make the most of each of the British annual celebrations, from mixing the perfect Valentine's Day rose petal martini, to making handcrafted advent calendars and Christmas wreaths. It was jam-packed with recipes and useful tips, games and costume ideas. But it didn't sell as well as was hoped, and was criticized for sometimes stating the obvious. It was a shame for Pippa, as it was the first time she had a public voice, and it was clear she was smart, funny and self-deprecating. In the introduction, she wrote, 'It is a bit startling to achieve global recognition before the age of thirty on account of your sister, your brother-in-law and your bottom.'

Nevertheless, she picked herself up, dusted herself off, and as well as continuing to edit and write *Party Times*, she also landed the job of columnist for *Waitrose* magazine which had previously been held by Delia Smith. She also continued to take more of an interested in the charity sector, supporting the Mary Hare School in Berkshire, who work with deaf children.

It was all change in her romantic life as well, and she had fallen for handsome stockbroker Nico Jackson. Unlike the men she had been out with in the past, he was grammar-school-educated and, after university, he had won a place on an M&C Saatchi graduate training scheme. He eventually switched to a career in the City, working for Deutsche Bank, which gave him an introduction into elite social circles. He and Pippa were first spotted together in September 2012 at the opening of former Boujis owner Jake Parkinson-Smith's new club 2 & 8, and five months later – in February 2013 – he was on holiday with Pippa and the rest of the Middletons, including pregnant sister Kate, in Mustique. Shortly after this sunshine break, Pippa was back to pushing herself physically. This time she had Nico as well as her brother by her side, when they all competed in the Engadin Skimarathon in the Swiss resort of St Moritz. Pippa completed the 26 miles in 2 hours 48 minutes – half an hour behind James and eight minutes behind Nico.

And what of the youngest of the Middleton clan? Born James William Middleton on 15 April 1987, he is the younger brother often overlooked by the media in favour of his older sisters. However, the dashing six-foot entrepreneur had also been working and playing in the capital for quite some time. He followed his sisters to St Andrews, and then to Marlborough, where he played in the second rugby XV and the first tennis team. He was also head of his house. He then followed Pippa to Edinburgh University to study environmental resource management, but dropped out after one year. Instead, he borrowed £11,000 from his uncle, Gary Goldsmith, to start up his own business. The resulting Cake Kit Company sold disposable kits that allowed customers to bake elaborate cakes at home, and later branched out to sell cookie dough, cupcakes and candles that smell like home-baking. As a dyslexic, James found academia difficult, but in business he had found his niche, and by the time the company had been running for a year, he had paid his uncle back all that he had borrowed. In 2010, James registered the names of three new companies – Nice Cakes, Nice Wine and Nice Group London – the last he hoped to grow into an umbrella company to turn into a business empire.

Nice Cakes personalized cakes including transferring

customers' photos in icing on to them. In 2011, he dropped a line of saucy products that included a 'Wonderful Wife' cake adorned with the slogan 'scrummy boobies that make my hands happy' and a 'Stud Muffin' design, showing an image of a man alongside the words 'a willy that wriggles and gives me the giggles'. He had previously raised eyebrows when pictures emerged of him half-naked and dressed in drag, and he'd been literally caught with his pants down after his twenty-first birthday party in 2008, when he was photographed urinating in the street. However, such youthful indiscretions soon became a thing of the past, and as the years went by, he matured into a more low-key young man. He focused on his business, kept bees, played tennis with his sisters and football with William, and walked his family's black cocker spaniel Ella – the mother of William and Kate's dog Lupo.

James had always managed to keep his love life fairly private, leading to speculation that we was gay, but a friend told the *Daily Mail*, 'If you've ever heard James talk privately about girls, you'd know he's not gay. But he's not that bothered by the rumours, either. He's quite "meterosexual" so, in a way, he takes it as a compliment.' His exes include a Miss Scotland called Katharine Brown who he dated during his year at Edinburgh University, a pretty blonde Australian called Amy Bradshaw, who he split from shortly before the royal wedding, an American interior designer who he was with for eighteen months, and Brazilian model and fashion design student called Fernanda. Like his sisters he has a close-knit group friends around him, and his plus-one at the royal wedding was society magician Drummond Money-Coutts.

In early 2013, after splitting up with model Emily Steel, James began a relationship with Donna Air and had his first experience of dating someone in the public eye. Donna was seven years his senior, with a nine-year-old daughter by casino owner Damian Aspinall, and had previously been linked with Calum Best. To many, the actress and TV presenter and the brother of the future Queen didn't seem like an obvious match, but Donna was already firm friends with Princesses Beatrice and Eugenie, and she and James both shared a passion for an active lifestyle. In the same year, James took part in a charity ski race, Donna ran a charity race for Jeans for Genes. She has also worked in conservation and champions organic food. The pair had only been together for a few months before they were double-dating with Pippa and Nico, enjoying a night out at new private member's club Loulous.

Historically, those who married an heir or heiress to the throne were required to put their own families on the 'back-burner'. Being a member of royalty was being part of a business, but it was also being part of a very structured and traditional family with very specific requirements. There would always be Easter at Windsor Castle, summer holidays at Balmoral, and Christmas at Sandringham, all of which were non-negotiable. Christmases with blood family often became a thing of the past.

However, this was not to be the case for Kate. She and William have spent more time with the Middletons than Charles and Diana ever spent with the Spencers, and the Spencers were certainly not embraced by the royal family in the way the Middletons have been. As well as Kate going on royal skiing holidays to Klosters with Charles and Harry, William also holidayed with Kate and her family in Mustique and Ibiza. Charles and Camilla were keen to meet Carole and Michael at Kate and William's graduation, and invited them to Birkhall after the engagement, while the Queen also welcomed them to the fold. They were twice guests at Ascot, sat in the royal box at Wimbledon, and James was invited to breakfast with William and Harry on the morning of the wedding. The whole Middleton family were part of the Diamond Jubilee River Pageant.

By the time Kate became a part of the royal family, slight changes in the more antiquated practices had already been made, and she was a beneficiary of this. It helped that William genuinely liked and cared for Kate's family, and they in turn saw him as a son. He paid tribute to Kate's parents in his engagement interview, saying, 'I get on really well with them and I've been very lucky they have been so supportive. Mike and Carole have been really loving and caring and really fun and have been really welcoming towards me so I have felt like one of the family.'

He also knew the importance of Kate not feeling cut off from the outside world and all that she knew, as his mother had felt as soon as her engagement was announced. He knew that for Kate to be a happy, fulfilled and useful member of the royal family, she would need to maintain her close relationship with her own family, adding, 'Her and her family – I really want to make sure they have the best guidance and chance to see what life's been like and what life is like in the family.' The fact that he not only wants Kate to be taken care of but her parents and siblings too shows the times really are a-changing.

CHAPTER TWELVE

Rowing into the
midnight sun

In the days after the wedding, people all around the country packed up their bunting and pored over pictures from the big day, while queues of those wanting to view the flowers snaked around the abbey. The morning after, Kate and William posed for their 'going away' pictures in the grounds of Buckingham Palace, and both looked fresh-faced and relaxed, with Kate in a blue Zara dress and Black Ralph Lauren jacket. They then took a helicopter to the Scottish Highlands for two days, before William was back to work. Just days after walking up the aisle of Westminster Abbey, Kate was back in the aisles of Waitrose in Anglesey, as she and William had decided to wait until the buzz of the wedding had died down a little before going away.

Kate's wedding bouquet was laid on the grave of the Unknown

Warrior in Westminster Abbey – a tradition the Queen Mother had started – and William carried out two rescues, including that of a seventy-year-old man who'd had a heart attack while climbing. The newlyweds then left for their ten-day honeymoon in the Seychelles a week later. Because it was a private trip, the destination was not going to be announced, but the ministry of tourism for the Seychelles confirmed it. The couple had been to the area three years earlier to cement their relationship after the breakup, and found it so utterly idyllic that they decided to return. The Seychelles is an archipelago of 115 islands scattered through the Indian Ocean, to the East of mainland Africa. One of the most remote is North Island, which they reached by helicopter after flying into the capital, Male. Their home for the next ten days was a private island with white sand beaches fringed with Coco de Mer palm trees and home to ancient giant tortoises.

The island resort is also an environment focused on conservation, with a turtle-nest monitoring programme in progress which means that at night the beaches are in darkness, lit only by moon and stars, so any hatching turtles don't head in the wrong direction. Kate and William stayed in a luxury villa costing £3,000 a night, and from the moment they arrived everything that happened was up to them – there are no set mealtimes as guests discuss food with the executive chef when they arrive, and can eat when they like. There is a wine cellar they can walk into and make their own selection, and the spa is always ready to open whenever the customer fancies a treatment. The whole island has been so beautifully designed, with sun-bleached wood and sea-smoothed stone that everything blends and complements the natural landscape – with wooden decks incorporated into trees, four posters with white muslin curtains, and sunken baths all half concealed by lush greenery. As well as padding around the island, Kate and William spent a lot of time diving, and came home with golden tans.

When they returned to Anglesey, William went back to work and Kate started preparing for her first royal tour in July, which would see the couple travel all over Canada before ending in Los Angeles. Before the tour, sporting her honeymoon tan and shell jewellery from the North Island boutique, Kate and William met with US President Barack Obama and his First Lady, Michelle, at Buckingham Palace. The Obamas were on a state visit to the UK, and wished the newlyweds well, telling the couple they had enjoyed watching their wedding on TV.

It was a summer of family fun as well as royal firsts for Kate, with celebrations for Prince Philip's ninetieth birthday, a day out in the royal box at the Epsom Derby, Garter Day at Windsor Castle, and Kate's first Trooping the Colour, when regiments of the British and Commonwealth armies march past the Queen to celebrate her birthday. She and William also went to see *Bridesmaids* and *Harry Potter and the Deathly Hallows: Part 2* in one sitting, in the Llandudno Cineworld, and attended their first black tie gala as a married couple.

The Absolute Return for Kids charity aims to promote health, education and child protection around the globe, and was set up by Uma Thurman's partner, Swiss financier Arpad Busson. Kate and William chose to attend the ARK fundraiser as their first glittering evening event after they were married, because their own charity the Royal Foundation would be working closely with ARK. Guests were paying £10,000 a ticket.

At the end of June, they embarked on their first tour together. It was dubbed the honeymoon tour and spanned a jam-packed eleven days where they zipped all over Canada. The country was chosen because the Queen is Canada's head of state, and therefore William one day will be too. The tour would end with two days in Los Angeles to raise money for charity and strengthen business links between the US and the UK. Kate had travelled through South America, the Caribbean, Europe, Africa and the islands of the Indian Ocean but she had never been to North America and was very excited about the coming few weeks.

A royal tour is put together to promote strong links between the UK and other countries around the world – for trade, business and good relations. Many places and activities are considered before deciding which are the best fit for the visiting royals. Events usually covered on tour include an official welcome where the royal party take the royal salute from the local military; meeting with prime ministers, governors, and overseas royals; paying their respects to those who have died for their country at war; and taking an interest in what is important to that particular country. On a personal level, the royals also like to include engagements which tie in with the charities they support.

There was a lot of speculation about how many people would be in the couple's entourage. Prince Charles often takes fifteen people including a watercolour painter. In the end, Kate and William took just seven. A private secretary, a tour coordinator, two press secretaries, an advisor, an administrative assistant and Kate's hairdresser. Kate did her own makeup and, instead of having a traditional lady-in-waiting, when she was on walkabouts one of the men from the entourage would help collect the flowers she received from well-wishers. In her small clutch she carried a compact mirror, blotting paper, handkerchief and lip balm, and since she had always been a keen photographer, she took her own Canon camera to snap some personal images.

It was an ambitious tour that covered thirty engagements across nearly 20,000 miles in eleven days. 'The pace was relentless,' recalls photographer Chris Jackson. 'Travelling across a country like Canada means crossing time zones and really subjecting your body to the stresses and strains of multiple flights and constant movement.'

On 30 June, the couple touched down in Ottawa and experienced a rapturous reception from the crowds who had been arriving since 5 a.m. They went straight to pay their respects at the Canadian Cenotaph, and the Tomb of the Unknown Warrior, where William laid a wreath and Kate laid a posy as a lone trumpeter played the last post. The pair then separated to mix with the crowds, with Kate occasionally looking over to William to make sure she was moving at the right speed, and as they climbed into the car afterwards, she leaned into his shoulder on the back seat. There followed the official welcome at Rideau Hall, the home of the Queen's representative in the country – the governor general – and an evening reception with young Canadians who had been selected because of their charity work. The next day, 1 July, Kate displayed her Middleton composure at the Canada Day celebrations.

For the midday concert, 300,000 people had turned out – some had travelled thousands of miles to see the royal couple and shouted, 'Will and Kate! Will and Kate!' the way that sports fans usually chant, 'USA! USA!' Many wore fascinators, which since the wedding had come to be associated with the new Duchess. In the ninety-degree heat, people were fainting and being passed over barriers. Kate respectfully wore long sleeves and a hat, but despite her makeup melting in the midday sun, she remained serene throughout the three-hour concert. On the day after, which was also the day after what would have been the Princess of Wales' fiftieth birthday, William and Kate took a cooler walk through the peaceful gardens of Rideau Hall where they stopped to take a look at the tree Diana had planted.

Next they headed east to Montreal. The French-speaking city has long been a challenging place for royals to visit, since many of the inhabitants do not wish to be ruled by the royal family. A small group of protestors had gathered to show their displeasure, but the cheers drowned out the boos, and the royals' spokesman later said, 'They considered the protests to be part of the rich fabric of Canada.'

The couple visited the Sainte-Justine university children's hospital, where they both sat in little children's chairs and spoke French to the young patients they met, and then travelled to nearby Quebec for a prayer service and visit to La Maison Dauphine, a centre which helps homeless youths. It would partly be her experiences on this tour with the children and young people she met that would lead Kate to focus on young people when she came to make her decisions about her charity patronages later in the year.

On the second part of their tour they started to look like best friends, as well as a couple in love. And in the rolling green hills and dainty beaches of Charlottetown they dressed down for the start of the more rough and ready leg of their trip.

William skilfully crash-landed a Sea King helicopter onto the lake (it was a move that wasn't a part of his training back home – he had never performed it before – but one that he could use on his return), while in a romantic gesture, he banked the helicopter in front of his new wife so she had a good view into the cockpit. They then took part in a dragon boat race on opposing teams, and although they are both sporty and competitive the pair showed quite different styles. One of Kate's teammates said afterwards, 'She was really quiet. I think she was feeling quite a bit of pressure because she has done it before,' while William shouted to Kate and her team, 'You're going down!' His team won by a third of a length, and the pumped-up prince said, 'There's no chivalry in sport!' as he was presented with a bottle of champagne, before wrapping his arms round his wife for a very public hug. Both rain-lashed, whipped by the wind, sprayed with lake water and laughing, it was clear they were thoroughly enjoying themselves.

Chris Jackson recalls, 'I often find on these tours that the more remote you go, the better pictures you get. You start to see some of the real characteristics that make this couple who they are. As they disembarked the dragon boats, an affectionate embrace in the drizzle was certainly the picture of the day and a rare show of real affection from this couple who are often so tied to formal and structured royal protocol.'

Afterwards they moved on to the sub-Arctic wilderness of Yellowknife, where they were welcomed by aboriginal people throat singing and playing drums, and Kate was presented with a polar-bear brooch made from locally mined diamonds. They met rangers who taught them survival techniques such as how to skin animals and smoke the meat. After spending the night there, on what was meant to be their day off they decided to visit Slave Lake – an area that had been totally devastated by a wildfire just two months earlier. They visited to see how the rebuilding was going on, and to talk the people about how they were recovering from it. For the final leg of the Canadian part of the tour, they flew into Calgary, and as they stepped on to the tarmac they were greeted by a little girl who became overwhelmed and ran into Kate's arms.

Six-year-old Diamond Marshall had an abdominal tumour and had watched the royal wedding from her hospital bed, wishing that she could meet a real-life duchess. When her family found out the couple were visiting, they wrote and asked if a meeting might be possible. On the day, it proved a bit much for the little girl as she dived in for a cuddle. William and Kate were then 'white-hatted' – the Western city's tradition where visiting dignitaries are presented with custom-made white cowboy hats – and headed for an evening business reception with a denim and cowboy boots dress code. They watched sheep-riders and when Kate saw a man in leather chaps she displayed the 'cheeky' sense of humour that William spoke of in their engagement interview, saying to him, 'We should get you a pair of those!' They finished their Canadian visit by attending the Stampede – the biggest rodeo in the world.

Moving on to Los Angeles, they mingled with famous Brits abroad David Beckham and Stephen Fry at a party thrown for them by the British consul-general. 'If you brought Clark Gable and Marilyn Monroe to life, Americans couldn't be more excited than they are by the presence of the Cambridges,' Stephen Fry said afterwards, 'Having them here is like fairy dust.'

William played polo to raise money for the Royal Foundation. Guests had paid up to $2,500 a ticket, and William didn't disappoint – scoring four goals for his team. Then in the evening they rubbed shoulders with Jennifer Lopez, Nicole Kidman, Tom Hanks and Barbra Streisand in the art deco Belasco Theatre. The event was hosted by BAFTA, of whom William is president, and was designed to help introduce upcoming British talent to Hollywood heavyweights. BAFTA vice-president Duncan Kenworthy reassured the guests before the couple arrived, 'When you meet them, you don't have to bow and curtsey. You can call them whatever you feel like: Your Royal Highness, sir, ma'am, William and Kate – just as the mood takes you.' They ate roast beef and rose meringues, and made a beeline for Sopranos actor James Gandolfini.

The next day they visited Inner-City Arts, which gives kids from poor neighbourhoods somewhere to express themselves. Kate took to an easel and painted a psychedelic snail, and she and William play-fought while they were leaving their hand-prints in clay. They then moved on to a jobs fair which aimed to help those in the forces to find work once they had left the military.

The newly-weds even managed to spend a little time alone together in Ottawa, taking a rowing boat out on to the lake by themselves, while in Yellowknife, William surprised Kate with a sunset picnic on a deserted island. The area is so far north that in the summer it never gets completely dark, and the couple had one of the best views of the incredible phenomenon of the midnight sun setting over the water, along with a feast of fish and caribou steaks cooked over a camp fire, while sitting on a white sandy beach surrounded by pink granite rocks. Near Calgary they also managed to slip off for some time together, spending a day and night in the Skoki Lodge in the Rockies – surrounded by flowers and with a glacier stream nearby, where they went walking among the valleys, lakes and towering mountains.

From her first bouquet of pink roses and thistles, to arctic posies and single blooms, Kate was given so many flowers that at the end of any engagement, those accompanying her were carrying armfuls. Since she and William were travelling thousands of miles during their tour it wasn't possible to get them all into vases, so she always kept a few for her and William's room that night, and the rest were delivered to local hospitals and hospices. Meanwhile, she and William also received a multitude of gifts – from a homemade crown, and a hand-woven tapestry of the couple kissing, to a knife and beaded moose-skin moccasins lined with beaver fur. They were returning with more than just memories. The couple would go on to use as many of the gifts as possible, displaying many in one of their official residences, and those they couldn't use straightaway were archived and kept in storage until a later date.

The couple returned to their farmhouse in Anglesey, but it wasn't now their only home. Since they were married, William had moved out of his apartments in Clarence House and Kate was no longer based in the Chelsea flat that was now being shared by Pippa and James. The new Duke and Duchess needed a London residence of their own, and after considering a few options they decided to return to the home of William's childhood – Kensington Palace. It had been a royal residence since the seventeenth century, when King William III bought it from the Earl of Nottingham. King William's asthma meant he needed fresh air, so rather than live on the banks of the Thames in Whitehall, he selected Kensington Palace, which was surrounded by gardens. An eighteen-year-old Princess Victoria was living there in 1837 when she woke and was told she was Queen, and later King George III had it turned it into several luxurious apartments to be used for the royal family, as well as 'grace and favour' apartments which were to be used by key members of royal staff, paying a minimal rent.

Charles and Diana had lived in Apartments 8 and 9 after they got married, and so it was the first home of William and

Harry, who had bedrooms there that they returned to in the school holidays until the time of Diana's death. Rather than return to the actual apartments where William grew up, he and Kate chose Apartment 1A, which had been the home of the Queen's sister Princess Margaret.

The only problem was that it needed extensive renovations. Until they could move in, they set up home in the understated property Nottingham Cottage, which was also part of the Kensington Place complex and had previously housed staff. It was a four-bedroom property, and although they employed a cleaner, the couple looked after everything else and didn't yet take on any domestic staff. When the couple were staying in London Kate shopped at the local Waitrose, tended to the small flower beds outside Nottingham Cottage and nipped around town in her blue Audi.

Between the 6 and 10 August, countrywide riots tore chunks out of England's major cities. London man Mark Duggan had been shot and killed by police during his arrest on 4 August and in the days that followed his local community in Tottenham protested. The action escalated into violent exchanges between police and the protestors, which then turned into the smashing, looting and torching of public and private buildings. Over the next few days, five people died and around £100 million worth of damage was done during copycat riots throughout the rest of London and cities including Birmingham, Bristol, Liverpool and Manchester. Anger as result of the country's economic decline was flagged up as one of the main reasons for the spread of violence, as the UK had been in a recession for two years and youth unemployment had risen. As the country began to piece itself back together again, public figures began to make visits to the badly affected areas to talk to the people there, and offer their support.

As representatives of their country, making the people affected feel like their country cared, Kate and William went to meet the parents of the three young men who died defending their community from looters in Birmingham. Haroon Jahan and brothers Shazad Ali and Abdul Musavir were killed when they were struck by a car as they tried to protect local shops. Kate and William also met with members of the emergency services who had helped and William comforted a woman who broke down when she was telling him about being attacked by the looters, encouraging her by saying, 'Don't let them beat you. You have gone through a terrific ordeal. Keep fighting. We will get them. I am here to help and here to listen to what you have to say.'

Kate was learning to balance her personal life with her public duties, and she privately researched which charities she was considering becoming a patron of. Although there was a never-ending spectrum to choose from, she knew that she would like to work with children, and she would like to make good use of her love and knowledge of the arts, as well as her passion for creativity. Her office began approaching assorted charities about potential ways that she could be involved with them. Because it was all new to her, she started from the ground and worked up. She made private visits to numerous organizations around the country, and did her own research for each. Tracy Rennie, the director of care for East Anglia's Children's Hospices, of which Kate went on to became patron, recalls, 'It was very clear she had done her research. She asked excellent questions and understood our organization. It wasn't someone who had just been briefed – she wasn't surprised about what we were telling her. She just knew it.' At that point, EACH was just one of the many organizations she paid a secret visit to, and for each one, she was as well-prepared, taking meetings with staff, being shown round facilities and talking at length to the beneficiaries of the organizations.

She also spent a lot of time with her new father-in-law Prince Charles, learning from him, and attending the ballet and opera. She and William attended the second royal wedding of the year when William's cousin Zara Phillips married rugby player Mike Tindall at Canongate Kirk, Edinburgh. She was also undertaking more engagements along with William, including one to the Royal Marsden Hospital. Visiting the Royal Marsden was Diana's first public engagement after she was married, and she became patron from 1989 until her death in 1997 before William took over as president in 2007. Kate and William met a little boy Fabian Bate, who was undergoing chemotherapy and Kate wrote him a letter afterwards, something she was doing more frequently as she met more people in the line of her work.

Her first solo engagement was as a stand-in for Prince Charles. He had helped set up In Kind Direct, which redistributes surplus goods from retailers and manufacturers to charities. He was due to attend the evening reception, but following the death of the Crown Prince of Saudi Arabia, he was required to fly there to offer the Queen's condolences, and so his 'darling daughter-in-law' filled in. She and William also made a brief trip to Copenhagen to visit UNICEF's emergency supply centre with the Crown Prince and Princess of Denmark. While they were there, they helped pack aid boxes which were heading to East Africa. Shortly afterwards, Kate attended her first Remembrance Day as a member of the royal family, where the senior members lay wreaths at the Cenotaph to remember those who have died for their country in wars. She attended the *Sun* Military Awards with William and Harry, and visited the Centrepoint Camberwell shelter with William.

In October 2011, it was announced that the rule of male-preference primogeniture was to be changed, which would mean that if Kate and William had a daughter before they had a son, she would be queen. Previously, a son would always have precedence over older female siblings. This was a historic change – bringing the law up-to-date for this future king and queen who are themselves expertly balancing tradition with modernity to help continue making the monarchy relevant today.

Now part of the royal family, Kate could now spend her first Christmas at Sandringham with the Queen and her family. A red-brick Victorian property, the Norfolk house was built in 1870 and is set in 20,000 acres of land that includes farms, woodland, and orchards, while the gardens are full of flowers, oaks, lakes, streams and grottoes. The Queen's father King George VI was born and died there, and it is known for its apple trees, which he had planted and which produce juice that can now be bought online.

Royal Christmases are very traditional. The Queen arrives a few days before Christmas Eve and supervises the last-minute preparations. In Kate's first year, the party was made up of the Queen and the Duke of Edinburgh; the Prince of Wales and Duchess of Cornwall; Prince Harry; the Duke of York and Princesses Beatrice and Eugenie; the Earl and Countess of Wessex and their children Lady Louise and James, Viscount Severn; the Princess Royal and husband Timothy Lawrence; Peter and Autumn Phillips, with their daughter Savannah; and Mike and Zara Tindall. After years of turbulence behind the scenes with unhappy marriages causing a strain, everyone was happy, and there was a broad cross-section of ages to keep things lively, from Prince Philip aged ninety, to Edward and Sophie's son James who had just turned four.

However, it wasn't to be quite the traditional Christmas that the family were anticipating as Prince Philip had been feeling unwell, and on the day before Christmas Eve he was airlifted to Papworth Hospital suffering from chest pains. He was found to have a blocked coronary artery and a stent was fitted, which although deemed a minor procedure meant that he was kept in the hospital over Christmas as a precaution. Although the family were understandably concerned, they were reassured by the hospital that he was doing well, and they proceeded with their Christmas plans without him. There were children to think of, and the whole family didn't usually get the chance to spend some time together, so they needed to make the most of it.

On Christmas Eve, the family always gather in the White Drawing Room – a long light room with trompe l'oeil ceiling panels painted to look like the sky, with pheasants and doves around the edges. The room has two fireplaces, and is furnished with cream silk Victorian sofas, marble statues, a piano and cabinets full of exquisite figurines made from jade, rose quartz and amethyst. All figurines are presents from throughout the years to four generations of the royal family. There are paintings on the walls and no overhead lights, just side-lighting provided by little lamps. There are floor-to-ceiling picture windows along the wall overlooking the lawn, and a ceiling-high Christmas tree – a Norfolk spruce felled from the estate and decorated by staff with Queen Victoria's angels and baubles. The Queen would have added the last handful of ornaments when she arrived.

Because there are lots of mirrors in the room, including

mirrored doors, and the insides of all the cabinets, the fairy lights and lamps are reflected back and everything sparkles. The family follow the German tradition of opening their presents on Christmas Eve, and each member has their own table covered with a cloth and piled with presents. Prince Philip usually starts proceedings and then everyone dives in and Princess Margaret's son Viscount Linley has described it as 'total uproar'. The older members of the family tend to get a lot of joke presents, while the children are lavished with gifts. Kate had been experimenting with making jams and preserves that year, and gave her own homemade creations of strawberry jam and plum preserve to the Queen. It was business as usual when the family gathered together for dinner later. The Queen arrives at 8.15 for her dry martini and, as Sarah, Duchess of York commented in her autobiography, 'You never let the Queen beat you down to dinner, end of story – to come in any later would be unimaginably disrespectful.' The Christmas Eve dinner is black tie, and would typically include items such as Norfolk shrimp, and lamb or game shot on the estate, followed by a pudding made from fruit also grown on the estate.

Christmas Day, as usual, was an early start. Everyone in the house wakes up to a stocking, and meets for a quick breakfast before church at 11 a.m. The family always walk to the church of St Mary Magdalene, which is on the Sandringham estate and dates back to the early sixteenth century. It has a silver pulpit, a Florentine marble font, a jewelled Bible and memorials to the Queen's family on the walls, but is an intimate church for the local community. The rest of the congregation are made up of people who regularly attend services there throughout the year, although those who want to attend the service on Christmas Day need to apply in the autumn so they can pass the required security checks. Inside is decorated with holly and a tree from the royal estate and, for the collection, the Queen, Philip and Charles give an ironed ten pound note each which is folded so the Queen's head faces out. It was Kate's first year in the royal fold, and her first Sandringham Christmas church service. For the occasion she wore a plum coat and matching Jane Corbett hat, with her new green amethyst Kiki Mcdonough earrings, which were her Christmas present from William. During the service, rector of Sandringham the Reverend Jonathan Riviere said, 'We pray for the Queen and the Royal Family, especially today we pray for Prince Philip and his continued recovery.'

After walking back to the house, there was mulled wine served in the White Drawing Room before lunch. The family eat in the adjoining dining room, which has walnut and mahogany panelled walls painted in 'Braemar green' – a pistachio green – and hung with Spanish tapestries. Standing in the centre is a mahogany table which can seat up to twenty-four and is set with silver candelabra, flowers and silver pheasants and partridges. They dine from a white and blue Copeland dinner service and drink from crystal engraved with EIIR. Menus – as they always are for the Queen – are in French, and they tuck into turkey with chestnuts, herb stuffing and cranberry sauce and all the trimmings. They also have their own bespoke crackers with novelties and jokes inside.

From start to finish, as always, lunch was eaten in an hour and a half so the family could move through to the saloon to watch the Queen's speech on TV at 3 p.m. The saloon is a much smaller room decorated in cream and earthy neutral tones, softened by Brussels tapestries on the walls, antique rugs on the floors and plants in the corners. The Queen Mother's chair is left unused, and there is usually a jigsaw puzzle on the go on a side table. The

TV is normally stored in a cabinet, but is brought out as they all gather round on sofas and chairs to watch in silence. There is always time in the afternoon to relax or go for walks with the option of afternoon tea, but this year William, Harry, Peter, Zara, Beatrice and Eugenie drove to see their grandfather in hospital. In the evening they gather together for a lighter dinner of cold cuts and boozy puddings, and afterwards relax and play games together. In the past, favourites have included Trivial Pursuits, Monopoly and Who Wants To Be A Millionaire. Nobody goes to bed before the Queen.

Boxing Day is as much tradition as the rest of Christmas, as the family always head out on a shoot. A buffet of kedgeree, bacon and eggs, cereals and toast is laid on to set them up for the day, and Prince Philip usually would have organized the shoot across the cold, muddy fields. He, Charles, William, Harry, Edward and Peter Phillips are all keen, but Andrew less so. The womenfolk follow along behind picking up the pheasants, partridges and the occasional duck, and they have lunch in the heart of the estate, as the family clusters around a paraffin heater to cook sausages, and heat soups while they drink warming shots of spirits and hot tea. This year, Philip was discharged from hospital in the morning and after thanking the hospital staff for looking after him, he was driven back to Sandringham to his family. Although he couldn't take part in the shoot that year, he joined them for lunch and was there for the rest of the festive season.

Her first royal Christmas enjoyed and over, Kate then welcomed in the New Year with her family and William at the Middletons' home in Bucklebury.

CHAPTER THIRTEEN
'Sledge'

To Kate, she was simply walking down the road to work, but to those looking at the pictures, the pavement was a catwalk and her style choices were scrutinized and emulated. The road outside Boujis was swiftly re-imagined as a red carpet; and when she popped to the shops it was the equivalent of a top model landing a big advertising campaign. By the time her wedding day arrived, the pictures splashed across the daily papers may as well as have been the front cover of *Vogue*. Without meaning to, Kate had become one of the country's number one style icons. Five foot ten inches tall and lean from her tennis, swimming and gym sessions, she was the perfect fashion plate. Websites were set up to chart her fashion choices, and they tirelessly worked on finding out where every single item she wore was from, piecing things together like fashion sleuths. The likes of www.whatkatewore.com not only charted every stitch of style choice but included detail of all her official engagements – reporting what she was doing and why in easily understandable bites of information.

She had been on the radar as soon as she clasped hands with William around her ski-pole – but after the engagement interest in her went truly stratospheric. She had been scattered through the pages of newspapers and magazines for six years, and although her style was often commented upon and copied, she didn't yet make front-page news. She mostly favoured Chelsea girl chic or classic country casuals, but during those six years she was slowly finding her feet style-wise, and when she suddenly became front page news again, and again, and again, she had by then found her look. This is when people properly sat up and took notice as if with new eyes, and the 'Kate effect' kicked in. Her look was very different to what had been popular in the mainstream over the past few years. After the boho-chic gilets and maxi-skirts of Sienna Miller and the high-lacquer and funky sexy glamour of Cheryl Cole, people were ready for something different. And all of a sudden, here was a young woman who favoured more elegant, ladylike looks but still had the tan and the big bouncy blow-dry which made her look young and full of life.

'I think everybody is always looking for new people to represent fashion in this country,' the editor of British *Vogue*, Alexandra Shulman, told the *Daily Telegraph*. 'So when you get a pretty young woman who's going to have an incredibly high profile, the inclination is to think she's a good thing and want to embrace her, and I think the fashion world has done that.'

She had been a late bloomer in the style stakes. At school she dressed down in jeans and pastel tops with pendants and bangles, her hair scraped back into a bobble. Her Uncle Gary was more interested in designer labels than his niece, and he had bought her a Gucci bag and expensive watches. By the time she went to university she alternated between preppy in boyfriend jeans and sports jumpers, and smart-casual in boot-cut denim, cashmere sweaters and tailored jackets. It was when she first moved to London that she started to find her way. After a brief transitional period in which she dressed a little old for her years, she modernized and revitalized her wardrobe, and people began paying attention to her style choices as much as her choice of boyfriend. The high street pieces she wore would immediately sell out. As frenzied speculation built in the run up to her twenty-fifth birthday about whether an engagement was imminent, she emerged on the day in a simple black and white Top Shop dress which cost £45. It had sold out the following day.

As a London girl about town, her style was all about three 'f's: feminine, floaty and flirty. She favoured floral prints and lots of white, cream and pastels. A simple outfit would be made more girlie with a small feminine detail – a ribbon-trim, a lace edge, a small bow or a frill – but never more than one per outfit. There would usually be a little flash of sex-appeal, whether it was a hint of cleavage, a nipped in waist, a figure-hugging wrap dress or bare legs with a golden tan. She mixed the elements together well and the overall affect was appealing to men and women. Her Chelsea girl chic involved summer staples such as French Sole pumps and white jeans, while in the winter or when she was in the country she favoured tweeds and tartans, brown suede boots and fitted jackets with a pelmet.

As well as shopping up the Kings Road, she also enjoyed hunting for bargains in TK Maxx and was a huge fan of the discount outlet mall Bicester Village for snapping up discounted designer labels. She respects the opinions of her mother and

Pippa – they have all borrowed each other's clothes on occasion, and it was Carole who introduced Kate to the countryside store Moda Rosa. Kate was delighted to discover that it stocked many of her favourite labels including Temperley, Issa, Jenny Packham, Diane Von Furstenberg and Libélula.

Although she had a couple of key expensive jewellery pieces, like her Asprey diamond button pendant and good pairs of diamond and pearl earrings, she wore a lot of dress jewellery including big dangly earrings and pendants set with semi-precious stones. Apart from her bags and Chanel sunglasses, not a lot of her wardrobe was designer – she favoured Reiss, Zara and Jigsaw from the high street. For the many weddings she started attending, she favoured silky slip dresses and tailored jackets with a fascinator worn on the side of her head, and unlike some tall women she has always been unafraid to opt for a skyscraper stiletto heel. For weddings in her twenties she went for more cleavage and less in her hair, which was reversed as she got older. There were of course some outfits that didn't work as well as others – at the Cheltenham Races 2006, she was swamped in a floor-length coat, baggy boots and large fur hat, for which she received additional criticism as it was made from mink. Twice at the same event the following year she wore a long-flared tweed skirt teamed first with a tweed jacket and then a paisley scarf and pashmina, which drowned her in fabric and overall led to an ageing effect.

However, two Boodles Boxing Balls first showed that she was capable of a jaw-dropping look. They were not what had come to be expected of her – bold colours, slashed down the front and form-fitting with nipped in waists and detailing to emphasize her femininity. In 2006, she opted for BCBG Max Azria and in 2008, for Issa. She also made more people than

William sit up and take notice with her breakup wardrobe, opting for a younger, sexier party-girl look with bold prints, bright colours, short skirts and midriff or bare shoulders on display. The summer brights and higher hemlines continued when she got back together with William.

The 'Kate effect' exploded with the dress she wore to announce her engagement. It was by one of her favourite labels – Issa, which had been created by Brazilian designer Daniella Helayel. The midnight-blue satin, Diana's sapphire, and a subtle lapis and diamond necklace teamed with the glossy brunette blow-dry, roses in her cheeks and sparkling eyes became the first iconic image of Kate. It wasn't to be the last. A wedding dress is for many women the most important dress of their lives – the one they spend the most money on, and the one they scrutinize on others. At the end of a big collection, fashion designers always send their muse down the runway in a wedding dress, and in Kate's case it was also a very obvious signifier of her achieving royal status. The ivory silk and lace creation even had its own exhibition and became her second iconic item of clothing.

Kate's style also changed slightly after the wedding – she still looked like herself, but a sharpened-up version. She started favouring more structured dresses, with generally longer hemlines and necklines cut higher. Now she had crossed over into royal status, she was seen in even more different situations than before – she would now be viewed in a succession of outfits including daytime formal, daytime casual, business meetings, church, action-ready, evening informal and black-tie. She had to get used to the many sartorial challenges, which inevitably seem shallow if spoken about at length, but still were all incredibly important to get right. After all, she would be criticized quickly enough if she slipped up.

The fact is appearances are important when you are a member of the royal family, and many factors have to be considered. There would be etiquette guidelines about what should be worn for certain events.

Following in the footsteps of senior royal women, she started wearing more bright colours, favouring blue the most, which she chose for her engagement dress, post-wedding going-away outfit, the first day of the Canadian tour, her first public engagement with the Queen, her first speech and for the day she left hospital after the announcement of her pregnancy. She knows the appropriate attire for various events – opting for tweed at the races, white for Wimbledon, green for St Patrick's Day, tartan on St Andrew's Day, daffodils in her lapel for St David's Day, and red, cream and blue for the Diamond Jubilee events. Royals don't usually wear black, and the Queen reserves it just for funerals, Remembrance Day and in the company of the pope; however, Kate broke with tradition when she wore a stunning floor-length, strapless black velvet gown for the *Sun* Military Awards in 2010, accessorizing with an impressive ruby necklace and matching bracelet and earrings. Most of the time she sticks to the rules but, confident in herself, she knows when she can bend them.

On tour she would be wearing around three outfits a day, and those outfits like it or not would need complementing accessories and jewellery. There would need to be standby outfits in case the weather changed or there was an accident, and many pairs of replacement tights.

It was especially of interest on the Canadian tour when pictures were constantly updated online every day for nearly two weeks. She wore more than twenty outfits in quick succession and, for some, she became seen almost as a dress-up doll.

What would 'action Kate' wear? Or 'ball-dress Kate' or 'cowgirl Kate'? With her royal status, however, came the responsibility of diplomacy, and with the help of royal advisors she carried it off with aplomb. When she took off for the Canadian tour, in a bow to Canada's historic links with France, she wore a French designer dress (Roland Mouret) and Canadian designer blazer (Smythe Les Vestes), followed by a dress by a Montreal-born designer (Erdem Moralioglu) for her arrival and official welcome to Canada. The following day, for Canada Day, she honoured the country's national emblem by wearing a red maple leaf hat and a diamond maple leaf brooch that had been presented to the Queen Mother on her first Canadian tour in 1939. Kate wore another Erdem creation in Quebec City, a nautical-inspired dress in the seaside town of Charlottetown, and cowboy boots with turquoise jewellery from a local designer Corrie McLeod to the rodeo in Calgary.

She then wore American designer Diane Von Furstenberg on her first day in the United States, however she also flew the flag throughout the tour for British designers including Alexander McQueen, Jenny Packham and Catherine Walker, as well as for the British high street with many LK Bennett accessories and a Whistles outfit. Such was the frenzy for Kate-related fashion items, that LK Bennett opened a flagship store in New York the following year and Reiss expanded significantly throughout the US. Mary Alice Stephenson, former fashion editor at *Vogue*, said, 'While she may be supporting British brands, the way that Kate dresses is very all-American, classic sportswear with a twist. Kate is championing new home-grown talent and breathing life into iconic, traditional British brands.' And she certainly did – although many British fashion brands had previously seen a decline in sales, six months after the wedding and Canadian tour, LK Bennett saw a fifteen per cent increase and Reiss a ten per cent increase. *Vogue*'s Alexandra Shulman commented, 'I think what she wears really does translate to cash, and that's a fantastic boost for the home industry.'

On her second royal tour, which would take place in Asia in 2012, Kate and William visited the Botanical Gardens in Singapore to view orchids that had been named after the Princess of Wales and themselves. For the engagement Kate wore a specially created blush coloured silk Jenny Packham dress which had been hand painted with orchids. The following day, she wore a silk violet-print dress by Singapore-born Prabal Gurung to an evening reception, and at a formal state dinner in Malaysia she had requested the national flower the hibiscus to be embroidered on to her Alexander McQueen gown. She also wore a dress by local designer Raoul, who had been one of the stars of Singapore Fashion Week. Hilary Alexander, fashion director of the *Daily Telegraph*, also noted it was not just the more obvious gestures that Kate was paying attention to, adding, 'Not only was her symbolism spot-on, but the cuts of her dresses were appropriate, too. The style has had a slight hint toward the national dress, such as the V-neck Jenny Packham. That was similar to the tops that you see women in Singapore wearing.' Kate even wore a Project D dress when she briefly touched down in Australia on the way back in a nod to the heritage of the label's designer, Dannii Minogue.

Sensibly, Kate listens to her elders – during engagements the Queen has been quietly paying her respects to those around her through her clothing choices for decades, and Kate has learned from her. Royal ladies often find designers they are comfortable with and stick with them. The Queen favours her own dressmakers Angela Kelly and Stewart Parvin, and in recent years she has become known for her colour-blocking, always accessorizing with black shoes with a two-and-a-quarter-inch heel and a Launer handbag. Her hats are mostly designed by Rachel Trevor Morgan and are never so broad that her face is covered, and she still likes wearing gloves by Cornelia James. Kate has followed the Queen's lead by buying several pairs of her own Cornelia James gloves, and wearing her own Rachel Trevor Morgan hat in a Diamond Jubilee visit to Nottingham with the Queen.

Meanwhile, Camilla, Duchess of Cornwall is a fan of Anna Valentine outfits, and Philip Treacy hats, and Sophie, Countess of Wessex is often found in Bruce Oldfield or Roland Mouret with Jane Taylor hats. It was Sophie who turned Kate on to the dress jewellery of Heavenly Necklaces, with Kate snapping up a pair of their earrings worth just £40 which she wore to the Diamond Jubilee service at St Paul's.

Kate herself has been finding her way, blending designers with high street finds, and becoming an expert at mixing and matching her items to make them last longer and get the most out of them. Alexander McQueen has become a clear favourite for many occasions. She had not worn any McQueen before her wedding, and chose the design house for her wedding dress after being recommended head designer Sarah Burton by a friend. Sarah Burton had also designed the wedding dress of the Duchess of Cornwall's daughter Laura. Kate has since called upon the fashion house for most of her full-length gown needs, as well as other items across the board including coats, day dresses, belts, bags and jackets.

For formal day dresses she often opts for Jenny Packham, Amanda Wakeley, Temperley and Reiss. For hats she tends to call on Jane Corbett and Sylvia Fletcher, for bags Anya Hindmarch and Emmy Scarterfield, and for jeans J Brand and Zara. Her trademark, however, is the LK Bennett 'sledge' heel, which she has worn at Diamond Jubilee events as well as in the jungle on tropical islands. She has also favoured LK Bennett for wedges, bags and coats. She also wears a lot of Stuart Weitzman footwear and bags that are stocked in Russell and Bromley. For jewellery she favours Links of London and Tiffany, but her favourite is Kiki Mcdonough, who has been designing jewellery for twenty-five years. Kiki's royal connections started out with the generation before Kate, when Sarah Ferguson chose a pair of her earrings for her engagement portrait. Diana also favoured Kiki's designs, and a generation later she has become Kate's favourite when it comes to earrings – some of which are straight from the store, and others made especially for her.

Kate's clothing budget now comes from her father-in-law Prince Charles. She is sent large numbers of free clothes every week, but has to send it back with a polite note as the royal family cannot be seen to be endorsing anything in exchange for gifts. Like most people, and also like many of the royals, Kate often wears the same outfit on different occasions. However, everyone from Dame Vivienne Westwood to Kelly Osbourne has weighed in on her style choices, with Dame Vivienne saying she should recycle her outfits more and Kelly saying she only wear things once. Wisely, Kate takes counsel from the Queen and her mum and does her own thing.

Her sartorial choices can also now be used to promote philanthropy, as she can also draw attention to certain issues by what she wears. She has championed the ethical clothing company Beulah London, which was set up in 2009 by William's friend (and the partner of her ex, Rupert Finch) Lady Natasha

Rufus Isaacs and her friend Lavinia Brennan. The two friends had visited India, where they worked with abused women who had been rescued from the sex trade. They taught English and sewing in refuges in the slums of Delhi and, soon afterwards, also launched the Beulah Trust, which helps fund the training of women who have been abused.

Kate also chose to wear an orange and purple Smarties bracelet that had been designed by musician Ed Sheeran's mother Imogen to one of her public engagements. Imogen had started designing eye-catching jewellery inspired by sweets after the funding was cut from a youth arts programme she was working for. East Anglia's Children's Hospices commissioned Imogen to make a bracelet and it was picked up on by the press. Even a British Legion jewelled poppy Kate wore to an engagement was duly listed and priced on the website What Kate Wore.

Kate doesn't usually favour ostentatious jewellery and some of her simple favourite pieces include a ring studded with garnets and pearls which are hers and William's birth stones, a pair of green amethyst Kiki Mcdonough earrings which were a gift from William, and her Asprey diamond-encrusted button pendant. Her jewellery is usually quite subtle and understated, so the effect is even more stunning when she pulls out all the stops, as with the ruby set at *The Sun* Military Awards, or the impressive set of diamonds which Prince Charles gave her when she got married. Comprising of a wide bracelet and dangly earrings, she wore them to the In Kind Direct event where she had stepped in to represent an absent Charles, and the royal gala premiere of *War Horse*. Another key favourite piece is the charm bracelet that was a wedding present from Camilla. It is hung with a simple silver disc and on one side is Kate's royal cypher (a curly C with a coronet) and on the other is Camilla's (a plain C with a coronet).

Elizabeth Taylor was famed for her violet eyes, Julia Roberts for her smile and Angelina Jolie for her pout. For Kate, her most famous asset is her glossy brunette hair. Since her late teens she has worn it long. It is naturally curly, and reverted back to its natural state in the humidity of the Borneo rainforest on the Diamond Jubilee tour of Asia. It's also how she used to wear it while she was at St Andrews – it wasn't until she moved to London and started going to Richard Ward for blow-dries that she became the queen of gloss and bounce. Her stylist James Pryce left the Richard Ward salon at the end of 2011, so she took Amanda Cook Tucker, who has cut William and Harry's hair since they were little boys, on the tour of Asia. She stopped working with James Pryce because after he left Richard Ward there was a 'no poaching' policy for six months. Kate clearly needed someone to travel with her for engagements during that time, and that was when she decided upon Amanda. She has experimented with fringes and a sun-kissed look, but has always come back to a vegetable dye and subtle low lights.

Kate is also blessed with good skin, and likes to promote a healthy glowing look. She received some criticism for wearing her eyeliner too harshly and pencilling in her eyebrows too thick and dark, but they have both since been softened. She favours Bobbi Brown products which she buys from Peter Jones department store on the Kings Road. In the past, she has perched on a stool to receive tips from the Bobbi Brown staff, and on various excursions she bought brown eye shadow powder in the 'saddle' colour to darken her brows and make them appear thicker, gel eye-liner in 'Espresso Ink', and nude lip-liner in 'brownie pink' and matching lipstick in 'sandwich tulle'. Her skincare routine is simple, she has used the three step Bobbi Brown anti-wrinkle set which includes eye cream, facial corrector and concealer, as well as Karin Herzog skincare and Nivea moisturizer. Camilla also introduced Kate to bee-venom facials from the Hale Clinic, and Kate had also been known to use the bee-venom mask at home. It freshens the skin and is known as a natural alternative to Botox.

CHAPTER FOURTEEN

Patron Kate of Cool Britannia

At the start of 2011, with the wedding just around the corner, the future of the royal family was rosy. A year later, and it was vividly painted with red, white and blue. Kate would naturally play a role in the forthcoming Diamond Jubilee celebrations, and as ambassador for Team GB and Paralympics GB, along with William and Harry, she would also be a very visible presence at the Olympic Games, which shortly followed. It meant that baby chatter would fade into the background as together they supported the Queen and the country. It was also another year of many firsts for Kate – her first charity patronages were announced, she undertook her first solo personal engagement, gave her first speech, sat for her first portrait and attended her first Buckingham Palace garden party.

On 5 January 2012 it was announced that Kate was now patron of four charities: the National Portrait Gallery; East Anglia's Children's Hospices (EACH); Action on Addiction, who provide support and education for addicts and their families; and The Art Room, an organization who help children with emotional and behavioural difficulties. She was also to start volunteering with the Scouts, which was fitting considering her past as a Brownie. She would be regularly volunteering with her local Anglesey division of eight to ten-year-olds.

Patronages are one of the key areas of importance for each member of the royal family. Over the years they support many assorted projects and initiatives where they are able to help raise funds and awareness by being associated with them. However, when they become patron of a charity, the connection runs much deeper, and is usually something that is very close to their heart. They will be a patron for life, and will help raise funds and awareness, not just for the chosen charity, but more generally in the area it aims to help, as well. The National Portrait Gallery was a natural progression for Kate following on from her history of art degree, while she is also passionate about photography and even toyed with the idea of taking it up professionally at one point.

Additionally, it was clear that Kate had always shown an interest in vulnerable children. Visits to the children's hospital and homeless centre for teenagers in Quebec and the inner city arts project in LA were all important parts of their previous year's tour. Although her interest could actually be traced back as far as her charity dragon boat racing during her break-up with William. Back then she was hoping to raise money for two children's hospices, and in the following years she was involved with the Starlight Children's Foundation and the Day-

Glo Midnight Roller Disco, which raised funds for a children's hospital ward. So it was no surprise that Kate's other three patronages were related to the youth.

Although Action on Addiction do not solely support the young, her interest in children's welfare was the reason she approached them in the first place. The charity's chief executive Nick Barton explained, 'She was interested in young people and she said that wherever she pursued that line, she seemed to very often end up with the subject of addiction.' Addiction as a subject was seen as a brave choice for a member of the royal family and, later, comedian John Bishop who, with Kate, launched a youth counselling service called M-Pact, for children with parents who are addicted to drink and drugs, said, 'I think it's great that the royals are tackling raw, ugly, dirty and difficult issues such as addiction. They could spend their time and money on the National Theatre and no one would think anything wrong with it. But this is about people shooting up in toilets. It goes against type. And it's fantastic.'

Before the whirl of official engagements kicked off, Kate and William attended the royal gala premiere of Steven Spielberg's film *War Horse*, and the following day she celebrated her thirtieth birthday with friends and family in the private dining room of a Kensington restaurant. As in many previous years, shortly afterwards she waved goodbye to William as he embarked on another training course. This time, however, she was not alone, as the pair were proud owners of a new black cocker spaniel puppy call Lupo, who was the offspring of her parent's dog Ella. William was to spend seven weeks undertaking helicopter training in the Falklands, and Kate was going to be busy while he was away. Not only was there the new addition to take care of, but Kate was throwing herself into her new work.

Her first solo engagement was on 8 February to promote the launch of a Lucian Freud exhibition at the National Portrait Gallery. The exhibition had been five years in the planning and came about to tie in with the Olympics and Jubilee year. It brought together works from all over the world, and Kate knew the importance of such an event. The gallery's director Sandy Nairne said of their association with the Duchess, 'It's completely delightful because she is a terrific person and I think she's a great role model, particularly to reach out to young people who I think otherwise we might not get to.' He also stressed the importance of how deeply she was already involved, adding, 'She is someone who is interested in other people. I have been with her on each occasion she visited and what I see is someone who really pays attention. It makes a huge difference to the people she meets, and what they feel about themselves and their work.'

On Valentine's Day, she received not only flowers from William, but dozens of cards and roses from children at Alder Hey Children's Healthcare Hospital in Liverpool. She was in the city to visit the hospital and also to look around an alcohol-free bar sponsored by Action on Addiction, called the Brink. Nick Barton recalled his meeting with her the previous autumn when they met to discuss the nature of addiction, 'She asked very intelligent questions. We get a lot of visitors and sometimes you think "that's not a very sensible question" but hers seemed to be things that she had thought about.' Before the end of the month she had also visited Oxford to see the Art Room's work at Rose Hill Primary School.

The next month she got into the swing of things with other members of the royal family and demonstrated an easy rapport. The Queen had never invited Diana to an engagement with her, but on the 1 March she invited both Camilla and Kate along to upscale grocers Fortnum & Mason, to see the refurbishments that had been made, tour the store and open the Diamond Jubilee Tea Salon. Kate was with the Queen again, as well as Prince Philip, when they went to Leicester for the first of the Queen's Diamond Jubilee visits, which would see the Queen crisscross the country to meet and see as many of her subjects as possible in her special year. Kate then played hockey with the Olympic team and accompanied Charles and Camilla to Dulwich Picture Gallery to view youngsters' creations as part of the work of The Prince's Foundation for Children & the Arts.

She also handed out shamrocks to the Irish Guards on St Patrick's Day, as has been royal tradition for over a hundred years, and then decided to give her first speech at a children's hospice called The Treehouse, which had been funded by EACH. She had expressed an interest in this particular charity because they not only work with the children and their families inside the hospices, but in the community as well. While she was there she spent some time with four-year-old cancer patient Mackenzie Cackett and his family, and when the little boy died later that year, Kate wrote to his parents to express her sadness at their news. 'For those who don't know much about this area, when you are talking with families whose child is dying, you have to have a great deal of confidence and also a great deal of empathy,' explains Tracy Rennie, the director of care for EACH. 'In this particular circumstance, she had taken such an interest, we asked the family if they wanted us to let her know.' She also showed exactly why she is so suited to her role, when she remembered that his particular interest was in SpongeBob SquarePants. Tracy explains, 'Once the child has died, the memories are the most important things and she was so wonderful with the people she met. She was very interested in them and for those families to have that memory, that is something special for them.'

In between engagements she had meetings with charities, and private tutorials about government, the media and the arts to help prepare her for her for the future, and in her spare time she walked Lupo in Kensington Gardens, met up with friends for lunch at the Bluebird restaurant, played tennis with Pippa at the Harbour Club, and swam in the pool at Buckingham Palace. When William returned, they celebrated with a skiing trip to Meribel with the Middletons and then went on a string of joint engagements including the premiere of *African Cats* in association with Tusk Trust.

Around the time of their first wedding anniversary at the end of April it was noted that she and William were the first future monarchs in 200 years who hadn't conceived in their first year of marriage. But they were in modern times, and both had other priorities before starting a family. William wanted to continue working as a search and rescue pilot, while both felt the need for Kate to adjust to royal life slowly. Additionally, they were both Olympic ambassadors, and were set to play key roles in the Diamond Jubilee celebrations, meaning the summer months would be busy for the pair. Then in the autumn they were heading off to Singapore, Malaysia and the South Pacific to represent the queen on their Diamond Jubilee Tour.

Kate attended her first Buckingham Palace garden party at the end of May, with the Queen, Charles and Camilla. The parties are held every year to reward those who have performed a public service. Then came the first of the two main events of 2012.

The jubilee celebrations fell over three days – 3 to 5 June – and marked the sixtieth anniversary of the Queen's accession to the throne. The river pageant was the jewel in the crown of the events – nothing like it had been planned for 300 years – but unfortunately, there really is no guarantee of the British weather, and although it was held in June, it was freezing cold, with wild gales, mist and needling rain. However, that wasn't going to stop the 1.5 million people who had lined the Thames to wave, cheer and shout, or the additional millions who held street parties up and down the country. And it certainly didn't stop the participants of the pageant, who included Olympic and Paralympic athletes and Second World War veterans. In an unprecedented move, Kate's family were a part of the celebrations – Michael, Carole, Pippa and James travelled on paddle steamer the Elizabethan along with Olympics chief Lord Coe and Prince Charles's former page Michael Fawcett.

Kate chose to wear a scarlet Alexander McQueen dress for the big day, with matching Sylvia Fletcher hat and the Royal Navy Submarine Service crest brooch, featuring two dolphins and a crown. She, William and Harry boarded the royal vessel the Spirit of Chartwell along with the Queen, Philip, Charles and Camilla, and travelled down the river half protected from the rain by the canopy overhead. Although a pair of gilded seats had been crafted for the Queen and Prince Philip, the pair, who were aged eighty-six and ninety-one respectively, stood the whole way. 'I don't think they went below at all, actually.' Princess Anne said later in the ITV documentary *Our Queen*. 'They would have felt that it would have been utterly wrong to not have been there.'

Philip was hospitalized with a bladder infection the following day; however, he had done his duty. He and the Queen had been stoic, grateful and proud.

The following day, Kate, William, Harry, Beatrice, Eugenie,

Peter and Zara were among those in the royal box for the Diamond Jubilee concert, which had been organized by Gary Barlow. Unlike the previous day, it was a warm and golden afternoon that melted into evening, and saw key performances from Stevie Wonder, Sir Tom Jones and Kylie Minogue. The Golden Jubilee concert ten years earlier had been held around the back of Buckingham Palace, in the garden. Gary Barlow had wanted this concert to feel more inclusive, so it was staged around the famous Queen Victoria Memorial at the front of the palace, which meant that thousands of people could fill the mall and enjoy the music and atmosphere.

Robbie Williams opened the show with 'Let Me Entertain You', and was followed by Dame Shirley Bassey belting out the appropriate 'Diamonds Are Forever', and Grace Jones hula-hooping through 'Slave To The Rhythm', before Sir Elton John performed 'Your Song' and the stage was bathed in fuchsia light. Kate was spotted laughing, joking and waving her Union flag with William and Harry during the concert, as comedians Rob Brydon and Miranda Hart took to the stage.

The Queen missed the beginning but arrived in time for the special performance of the Diamond Jubilee single 'Sing', with singers and musicians from all over the world performing along with the Military Wives Choir. The whole of Buckingham Palace was projected with petals while classical singers Alfie Boe and Renée Fleming performed 'Somewhere', and then a row of houses was projected as Madness took to the roof to sing 'Our House'. The show was closed by Sir Paul McCartney, who roused the crowd into massive singsong of 'Ob-La-Di, Ob-La-Da', while a Union flag was projected on to the front of the palace, and an apocalyptic fireworks display exploded all around. The Queen and Charles then took to the stage with all the performers as Charles paid tribute to his mother, and his father in hospital.

Despite Kate and the younger members of the family then socializing at the after-party, where Carole Middleton told Cheryl Cole that she had the 'Middleton dimples', they all needed to be up early the next morning for the Service of Thanksgiving at St Paul's Cathedral. Afterwards came the culmination of the whole jubilee celebrations – a Buckingham Palace balcony appearance from the key members of the royal family. Where usually the balcony was packed with many members of the Queen's immediate family including her children, their children, and her cousins, this time there was a very stark difference. With Philip still in hospital, the group contained just the Queen, Charles, Camilla, William, Kate and Harry. Her message was clear – this is the stripped-down royal family, the royal family of the future. The Queen was flanked by Charles and William – the first and second in line to the throne.

The royal family were riding high. There had been a decade of sadness and change, but things were good again. They were all happy and the future looked positive. William was used to having the weight of his future weighing heavily on him, and had at times been understandably daunted by it, but now he had accepted his fate and was enjoying his life with Kate at his side.

The rest of the summer was taken up with the Olympics and Paralympics. Kate was there with William and Harry as the Olympic flame passed by Buckingham Palace (the Queen and Prince Philip saw it pass through Windsor Castle), and she was there alongside the Queen, William and Harry for the stunning opening ceremony. Those in the stadium witnessed first-hand the towering industrial chimneys rising from grassy pastures, the hundreds of illuminated NHS beds bouncing with children and the Olympic rings raining down fire showers.

However, the Olympics weren't just about the spectacle of the opening ceremony, and over the coming weeks Kate attended events on most days to lend her support to the GB athletes. She was there to watch William's cousin Zara ride to victory in the eventing and she also watched the tennis, cycling, track, hockey, swimming, gymnastics, handball, sailing, boxing and synchronized swimming. She visited the Team GB house and met Sophie Hosking, the gold-medal-winning rower, and not only did she attend events with her husband and brother-in-law but she went to the sailing with Princess Anne and the boxing with Anne's husband Timothy Lawrence as well. It was in the velodrome after Sir Chris Hoy raced to victory that she and William leaped to their feet for a hug, and they were there with Harry for Super Saturday when Jessica Ennis, Greg Rutherford and Mo Farah all won Olympic gold for Great Britain.

With the Queen taking some time out for a well-earned summer break in Balmoral following the months of Diamond Jubilee activities, and William serving with his search-and-rescue team, it fell to Harry to be called upon as the senior royal for the closing ceremony. He was accompanied by sister-in-law Kate. It was very significant that Harry was the senior royal there as it showed how much the Queen was beginning to trust him.

For the opening of the Paralympics, two-and-a-half weeks later, Kate sat between William and Anne, and over the next twelve days she attended cycling, goalball, rowing, athletics and swimming. She was there with William to see cyclist Sarah Storey win Team GB's first gold medal on day one, along with Sophie, Countess of Wessex, and her daughter Lady Louise

Windsor, who sat next to Kate. She was also there for day one's second gold, thanks to Jonathan Fox in the men's 100-metre backstroke.

Now her public duty was done, it was time to think about her less official duties, which luckily tied in with what she wanted herself. It was time to start trying for that baby which had been on people's minds since even before the kiss on the balcony the previous year ...

CHAPTER FIFTEEN

Invasion of privacy

C harles and Camilla headed for Australia, New Zealand, Papua New Guinea and Canada; Prince Harry whipped around Belize, the Bahamas and Jamaica; Prince Andrew went to India; Edward and Sophie visited a string of Caribbean islands; and Princess Anne travelled to Mozambique and Zambia. The Queen had crisscrossed the country, visiting as many places as possible during her Diamond Jubilee year, attending tea parties and country fairs, and so she left it to the younger members of her family to represent her overseas.

Kate and William were heading East, and it was unfamiliar territory for both of them. It was the first time either had been to Singapore, Malaysia, the Solomon Islands or the tiny, remote South Pacific island of Tuvalu. As usual their engagements were decided upon carefully, and the first, on 11 September 2012, was in Singapore.

They headed to the botanical gardens to view an orchid which had been named after them, as well as one which had been named after William's mother Diana. She had died before she got the chance to see it herself. Most of their engagements related to taking an interest in what was important to the country they were visiting, and attending formal receptions where they met state figures and local businesspeople. In Singapore they visited a pioneering housing estate and a cemetery of war graves, in Malaysia they had an official lunch with the prime minister and attended a glittering evening reception with the rulers of the country, but then came news from back home.

Just before the tour, the pair had borrowed the home of Viscount Linley in Provence for a short break, and unbeknown to them a local paparazzi had taken a set of pictures of Kate sunbathing topless on the balcony. The pictures had run in the French version of *Closer* magazine, and as the days span on, one publication after another printed them: in Denmark, Italy and Ireland. The editor of French *Closer* Laurence Pieau defended her decision stating, 'These photos are not in the least shocking. They show a young woman sunbathing topless, like the millions of women you see on beaches.'

A woman sunbathing topless on a public beach with a reasonable expectation that she might have her picture taken was one thing, a woman who presented a certain image of herself, due to her being a representative of her country, and who was photographed on private property was another.

The couple swiftly drafted one of the most strongly worded statements they had ever released: 'Their Royal Highnesses have been hugely saddened to learn that a French publication and a photographer have invaded their privacy in such a grotesque and totally unjustifiable manner. The incident is reminiscent of the worst excesses of the press and paparazzi during the life of Diana, Princess of Wales, and all the more upsetting to the Duke and Duchess for being so. Their Royal Highnesses had every expectation of privacy in the remote house. It is unthinkable that anyone should take such photographs, let alone publish them.'

Irish *Daily Star* editor Michael O'Kane argued of his decision to run the pictures: 'The Duchess would be no different to any other celeb pics we would get in, for example of Rihanna or Lady Gaga.' This seemed perhaps the weakest argument of all, since although Kate made a decision to enter into public life, it was a decision based on the fact she simply fell in love with someone who was in the public eye. She had not set out to be famous. Rihanna and Lady Gaga chose to take their clothes off on stage and in music videos to draw attention to their work, and Kate did not. Kate represented her country and her charity organizations, and so it was inappropriate that she would photographed in this way. Thomas Roussineau, who specializes in privacy law, summed up the action of taking the photos, telling the BBC, 'It is totally forbidden. The castle is not the street, it is in a private place. And they are intimate pictures.' In Kuala Lumpur, Kate boiled inside but she smiled for the cameras and took legal action.

However, it was business as usual – she and William visited a mosque in Kuala Lumpur. Kate continued to showcase an array of exquisite dresses in watercolour shades, and in the soupy heat attempted to stay cool with fans, paper parasols and wet wipes. The couple then headed off on the more rustic half of their trip. In the Borneo rainforest they were strapped into a seat to scale a tree – wearing khakis and with her hair curly with the humidity,

Kate may have been feeling vulnerable and angry, but she looked relaxed and as if she was enjoying herself. She explored the area with her camera, later displaying her pictures on the couple's official website. In the islands of the Pacific, where they headed next, she opted for bright tropical colours, floral prints and bold patterns however, they were all teamed with her trusty nude LK Bennett heels. She was gifted with a necklace made from dolphin teeth, shells and money, went to church and danced in a grass skirt.

She and William stayed in a luxury leaf-thatched bungalow in a bamboo four-poster bed, with an outdoor shower and a jetty overlooking the sea where they had breakfast the next morning – bacon and eggs for William, and scrambled eggs with smoked salmon for Kate. They drank pina coladas and in their private time went snorkelling.

The tour had been a huge success, and was the icing on the cake of what had been a triumphant jubilee year. Kate had remained silent about her thoughts on the topless pictures, and sure enough the story went away. The legal action, however, rumbled on.

In the last few months of the year, she and William lined up a few official engagements relating to his patronages – to the FA's new national football centre St George's Park in Staffordshire and to watch Wales play New Zealand at the Millennium Stadium in Cardiff. They also celebrated the 600th anniversary of St Andrews University, and Kate spent St Andrew's Day at her old prep school, playing hockey in heels, engaging in games with the children and opening the new sports facilities. Then shortly afterwards, when she was staying with her parents at their new home in Berkshire, she fell ill.

It was the news that everyone was expecting ... and yet not. Kate was only around four weeks' pregnant when she was rushed to hospital with *hyperemesis gravidarum* – a rare form of extreme morning sickness which meant it was impossible to eat or drink. She spent three nights in King Edward VII Hospital, where she was put on a drip, and visited by William, her parents and Pippa.

Royal pregnancies were not usually announced until after the three-month mark, after the biggest chance of miscarriage had passed, but in this instance it had to be announced when she was admitted to hospital. The people in the hospital needed to focus on doing their job rather than trying to keep the less scrupulous members of the press at bay, and so it had to be a case of full disclosure to prevent wild speculation, leaks, stress and distraction for people who had important jobs to do. It was a far from ideal situation and the couple were just getting used to the news themselves and many people close to them, including the Queen and Prince Charles, hadn't yet been told the happy news. It was such incredibly early days.

The King Edward Vll Hospital has treated many royals, including the Queen. All rooms are the same, so whichever royal is admitted will take any room available. They all have flat-screen TVs and access to a DVD library, and the patient can request the food they want. And so Kate found herself staring at a similar plain ceiling and walls to those found in hospitals across the country, but this one had pale blue floors with the royal ER crest on them.

She was tended to by consultant Alan Farthing, who is based at several London hospitals including St Mary's, which was where Kate was due to give birth. He was consultant obstetrician and gynaecologist, and was appointed to the Queen's royal medical team in 2008. Kate was also tended to by Marcus Setchell, who had spent two decades as the Queen's surgeon.

As Kate started to respond to the anti-sickness medication, she started to feel a bit better, and William came to visit every day. Outside, the television broadcasters, radio stations, newspapers and magazines churned with the news. They mostly reported the news straight – there was already enough drama going on with the shock announcement and hospitalization without another twist needing to be added. However, a small element were deciding what new angle they could give their coverage to go beyond the standard headlines.

On the other side of the world, producers at Australian radio station 2Day FM decided to call the hospital to see how close they could get to Kate. Mel Greig and Michael Christian called the hospital pretending to be the Queen and Prince Charles, and to their shock they were actually put through to a nurse, who transferred them to another, and they were able to ask a few questions. It was a shocking breach of security, and an invasion of privacy, but the couple took it in their stride. Later, when the real Prince Charles was asked his opinion about the royal baby, he raised his eyebrow and said, 'How do you know I'm not a radio station?'

However, then came truly shocking news, as it appeared that the nurse who had first answered the phone had committed suicide. Mother of two Jacintha Saldanha was found near to the hospital. As her family tried to come to terms with their loss, her former employers were quick to pay tribute, saying, 'Jacintha has worked at the King Edward VII Hospital for more than four years. She was an excellent nurse and well respected and popular with all of her colleagues.' It was thought the hospital had not been taking any action over what had happened, and Kate's press team let it be known that she had not made a complaint about the call, adding, 'Their thoughts and prayers are with Jacintha Saldanha's family, friends and colleagues at this very sad time.' All those affected by the events were left reeling.

When Diana was five months pregnant, she attended the funeral of her beloved godfather grief-stricken and alone. It was against protocol for members of the royal family to attend funerals if they weren't directly related, and so Charles stayed away. William showed how far the family had come when he prioritized his wife over a military engagement, three days after Kate returned home from hospital.

It was another significant change when he and Kate then spent Christmas 2012 with the Middletons. Senior members of the royal family had never been permitted to be anywhere other than Sandringham on Christmas Day in the past, so it certainly displayed how much times had changed.

This was the first time William got to see how his wife had always spent Christmas, although the Middletons were still settling into their new home. They had bought the grade II listed Georgian manor for £5 million earlier in the year and had been working on renovations. It was only the third property Carole and Michael had owned in their married life, and, even though their children had flown the nest, with seven bedrooms they would always be welcome. Its eighteen acres, with a swimming pool and tennis court, ensure that visitors would never be short of activities – and there were even outbuildings that would be transformed for Kate and William's protection officers.

Kate and William did still follow royal protocol by attending a church service at nearby St Mark's church in Englefield, and they joined the royal family for a pheasant shoot on the Sandringham estate on Boxing Day, although Kate and the Queen (who was shaking off a cold) stayed behind in the morning and joined the others at the smaller property Wood Farm for lunch.

CHAPTER SIXTEEN

Blooming

During the swinging sixties, Princess Margaret lived in Apartment 1A in Kensington Palace. It was painted pink and cornflower blue, and she played host to the likes of the Beatles and the Rolling Stones, Mary Quant and Vidal Sassoon, while Rudolf Nuyreyev, in skin-tight leather or a full-length fur coat, was not an uncommon sight. Apartment 1A will also be home to William and Kate for the foreseeable future and they will start creating their own unique memories there. Since Margaret's death and before Kate and William could move in, as well as modernizing and repainting, the living quarters also needed rewiring, the installation of new plumbing and the removal of asbestos. Around £1 million was spent, and the administration and refurbishments surrounding the move took nearly two years.

The four-storey apartment has twenty rooms including a dining room, study, garden room with floor-to-ceiling windows and a fireplace, reception rooms that can hold 100 people, staff quarters and a nursery. Outside is a walled garden flourishing with roses. Princess Margaret had once remarked, 'It's hard to believe one is in the middle of London.'

For the first two years of their marriage, Kate and William had been able to continue their lives much as they had before. They were based in Anglesey while William worked, Kate kept house and attended meetings and they enjoyed their simple life. However, 2013 was the time to change. Not only was there a baby on the way, but they were to move into their new home in the summer. Because it was a larger property, and because William would be giving up his job to become a full-time member of the royal family, they would now need staff.

Their offices were also transferring from St James Palace to Kensington Palace. Throughout their teenage years, William and Harry lived in Clarence House with Charles. His offices were also based there. So if there was a statement released, it would come from Clarence House. When William and Harry entered their twenties and started taking on more royal responsibilities and charities, their offices were based in nearby St James's Palace. However, when Kate and William married and moved into Nottingham Cottage in Kensington Palace, Harry soon followed, taking another apartment there. Kate and William were just waiting to move into 1A and then Harry could move into Nottingham Cottage. As William, Kate and Harry are all looked after by the same staff, the offices were moving too.

Kate's private secretary is Rebecca Deacon, daughter of a female priest and an Army major. She had worked as an assistant to the producers of the Diana tribute concert, and had also worked for Harry's Sentebale charity. She is a year younger than Kate and her responsibilities include helping with research, organizing her diary and assisting with her wardrobe. In the past, a female member of the royal family may have had a private secretary, a dresser and a lady in waiting, but Rebecca fulfils many of these duties, and Kate is very hands on herself. Kate chooses all her own clothes but Rebecca helps her to organize her wardrobe and is also on hand to offer advice. She accompanies Kate on all public engagements and is a support in every way.

Kate and William also have a personal private secretary, who is dedicated to dealing with the couple on a day-to-day basis. She makes travel arrangements, deals with private correspondence, books dentist and hair appointments, and looks after their private diary, including holidays and transportation. Kate still also has three private detectives.

William's private secretary is Miguel Head – he was previously press officer to William, Kate and Harry, and before that was press secretary for the Ministry of Defence. He was highly respected in his dealings of Harry's first tour of duty in Afghanistan, and was taken on permanently afterwards. They are also advised by Sir David Manning who was originally appointed by the Queen. He is the former British ambassador to the USA and had been at the foreign office for thirty-six years. His role is to share his knowledge of government and international relations as William, Kate and Harry move further on to the national and international stage. Their press officer is Ed Perkins, who came over from Buckingham Palace, and their assistant press secretary is Nick Loughran, who also moved over from the Ministry of Defence.

The couple were not just taking on new staff, but waving goodbye to a familiar face and one who had been an invaluable trusted friend and advisor for seven years. Jamie Lowther-

KATE

Pinkerton was private secretary to William and Harry when they were starting out in public life and had moved up to become head of their household. However, it was time for him to move on, and he would remain in their lives in an unofficial and still much respected and loved capacity.

After building a strong team around them, Kate and William turned their minds to domestic staff, and set about searching for a butler, cook and cleaners. As housekeeper, they employed Antonella Fresolone, who had been one of the Queen's housemaids and was at Buckingham Palace for thirteen years. She is now head of Kate and William's domestic staff and is in charge of cleaning, laundry, silverware and glassware.

Refurbishments were also under way on a ten-bedroom Georgian home called Anmer Hall, which stands on the Sandringham estate. Like other senior members of the family, the couple would need a country home as well as the Kensington Palace city dwelling, and this was given to the couple by the Queen. The Duke and Duchess of Kent used to live there, followed by the van Cutsem family, so William had visited his friends there many times when he was growing up. Planning permission for some alterations was granted, and architect Charles Morris, who had also worked on alterations at Highgrove, was appointed to add a new garden room onto the kitchen and convert a wood store into living quarters for protection officers. More trees will add privacy to the garden and a pergola is to be added to the patio.

The Queen has over 600 patronages, Philip has over 700, Charles over 600 and Anne 300. In thirty years' time, some of these royals will not be around any more. Where the Queen had four children, Charles had just two, and so there's no way the work could be split between his two sons and their two wives (when Harry marries), so the idea of the Royal Foundation came about.

The Foundation of Prince William and Prince Harry was set up in 2009, and in 2012, the name was changed to the Royal Foundation of the Duke and Duchess of Cambridge and Prince Harry. An umbrella charity to kick-start certain projects and cast light on others, it also means the three young royals have their own money to distribute as they wish. There are three main areas they chose to focus on: helping young people in society; raising awareness and support for the Armed Forces; and supporting communities to protect and conserve their natural resources for future generations. These objectives can be seen in many of the public engagements they undertake throughout the year, and in the areas they focus on when they visit overseas.

Of Kate's engagements, supporting young people led to her attending the launch of the Coach Core project, which aims to train the next generation of sports coaches, and to visit children camping out as part of the ARK Foundation's schemes. To raise support and awareness for the Armed Forces, she attended the *Sun* Military Awards; and to promote conservation she went to Grimsby, where she learned about sustainable fishing, and visited the rainforest in Borneo as part of the Diamond Jubilee tour.

In 2013, the foundation also took over the Diana, Princess of Wales Memorial Fund. The fund closed as a staffed operational organization on 31 December 2012, by which point it had raised more than £105 million. The Royal Foundation now have legal ownership and they will decide how to apportion the money which continues to be donated in Diana's name.

The Royal Foundation is a thriving charity, and raised

£4.8 million in 2011 compared with just £629,000 in 2010, before William and Kate announced their engagement. Meanwhile, £1 million more was raised by the American wing of the charity which was boosted by the polo match William played in during their first tour.

Twice a year, representatives from the charities of which Kate, William and Harry are patron gather to see how they can learn from and support each other. It's called the Charities Forum, and is a pioneering move that was dreamed up by William, and has so far been hugely successful. Kate, William and Harry are usually present, and it is held around a round table with about forty people followed by an informal reception. Because of the forum, EACH were able to collaborate with the Art Room on Christmas cards in 2012 – the cards were designed by children who had benefitted from the Art Room and EACH sold them to help raise awareness of and funds for both charities. EACH was also put in touch with Child Bereavement UK, of whom William is a patron, in the hope that they will work together in the future.

Kate celebrated her thirty-first birthday in January 2013 by going to see the Cirque du Soleil show *Kooza* at the Royal Albert Hall with William, her family and a selection of friends, but her first public engagement following her hospitalization and news of her pregnancy was to unveil her official portrait at the National Portrait Gallery two days later. Not many galleries commission new art, but the National Portrait Gallery is one of the few. Every year they commission a new portrait, and at the end of 2011, a long-time associate of the gallery Sir Hugh Leggatt approached them as he had been left some money by the recently deceased art collector Sir Denis Mahon and he wanted to used it to commission a portrait of Kate.

The gallery considered a selection of painters and discussed them with Kate before deciding on Glasgow-born Paul Emsley, who grew up in South Africa and won first prize in the BP Portrait Award in 2007. He had previously painted Nelson Mandela. Kate sat for him twice – once at Kensington Palace and once at his studios. Tellingly, following on from her wedding day, when she wanted to look natural and like herself, she said something similar to the artist. Paul Emsley says, 'The Duchess explained that she would like to be portrayed naturally – her natural self – as opposed to her official self. She struck me as enormously open and generous, and a very warm person. After initially feeling it was going to be an unsmiling portrait, I think it was the right choice in the end to have her smiling – that is really who she is.'

The portrait divided critics. Kate called it 'amazing' and 'brilliant', while art critic of the *Daly Mail* Robin Simon wrote, 'Thank goodness the beautiful Duchess of Cambridge does not look like this. I am sorry to say it is a rotten portrait.' However, William said it was 'just beautiful' and Richard Stone, who has painted members of the royal family for over three decades, thought it had, 'a lovely informality about it' and 'warmth'.

In February 2013, there was more controversy as Booker Prize-winning author Hilary Mantell gave a *London Review of Books* lecture about the role of royal women, opining: 'Kate seems to have been selected for her role of princess because she was irreproachable: as painfully thin as anyone could wish, without quirks, without oddities, without the risk of the emergence of character. She appears precision-made, machine-made ...' While some of what Mantel said in the lecture was taken out of context, and she was at times musing on the media's portrayal of Kate, there were many disparaging remarks made about her, and this particular portion managed to criticize all parties: the royal family by insinuating Kate had been selected for her role of wife based on cold, calculating factors; the Middletons for producing this person; and Kate herself. It was a perfect example of someone who has never had any interaction with Kate, making opinions based on very little evidence …

CHAPTER SEVENTEEN

Royal Princess

Following Mantel's remarks, Prime Minister David Cameron leaped to Kate's defence, describing her as: 'someone who's bright, who's engaging, who's a fantastic ambassador for Britain'. On the same day, Kate visited Hope House, an Action on Addiction-run residential home for women with addiction problems. Here she spent time talking with residents. 'We're dealing with people who have very low self-esteem,' explains Nick Barton, Chief Executive of Action on Addiction. 'And the fact that someone of this profile is prepared to come and spend time with them and talk to them, listen to them, hear their experiences. It makes them feel, "Gosh, maybe I am worth it." They all found it a terrific boost – as did the staff. The staff work very hard and they don't always get a lot of thanks or recognition from across the world, so this is a way of saying you're valued too, which is important.' It was the first time Kate's growing four-month bump was on display and although it was still just February, she chose to not cover up with a coat, but wore a bump-enhancing wrap dress.

With the crippling morning sickness behind her, instead of slowly winding down to the birth of her first child, Kate increased her workload and, after taking meetings and making a number of visits, it was announced that she was taking on three more charity patronages. One was an organization she had previous experience of – Place2Be, the youth counselling service that had benefitted from the Day-Glo Midnight Roller Disco attended by Kate five years earlier. The second was Sportsaid, which helps support up and coming athletes, and has in the past provided funding for numerous youngsters who went on to become Olympic champions, including Sir Bradley Wiggins, Sir Chris Hoy and Sir Steve Redgrave. The third was the Natural History Museum, which was another good fit considering Kate's love of the natural world, and the dedication of the Royal Foundation to preserving it. She had already undertaken an engagement there at the end of the previous year when she unveiled their new Treasures gallery.

Over the next four months, Kate travelled the country on public engagements, visiting Grimsby, Buckinghamshire, Cumbria, Glasgow, Ayrshire, Windsor, Manchester, Hertfordshire and Winchester. In Grimsby, she promoted the Princes Trust, and in London, she marked the 150th anniversary of the London Underground by visiting Baker Street tube station with the Queen and Prince Philip. In Scotland, she and William visited the Emirates Arena in Glasgow, where the Commonwealth Games will take place and, in Ayrshire, joined Prince Charles at one of his pet projects – Dumfries House, an outdoors centre for children.

Kate supported William at events relating to two of his patronages – visiting the Child Bereavement UK offices and, as he is the president of BAFTA, taking the Harry Potter tour at the Warner Bros. studios in Watford.

She also packed in many engagements relating to her own charities. As patron of East Anglia's Children's Hospices, she recorded her first public message to raise awareness for Children's Hospice Week, explaining, 'Children's hospices provide lifelines to families at a time of unimaginable pain. The support they give is vital. In order to carry out this wonderful work, our help is needed. With our support, those providing children's palliative care can continue to offer these extraordinary services. It does not bear thinking about what these families would do without this. With your support, we can help ensure that these children and their families can make the most of the precious time they have together.' It was a poignant and concise message, and one that she underlined when she made a visit to Naomi House, a children's hospice in Winchester.

She visited a Manchester primary school, The Willows. 'We were working with the Royal Foundation and Comic Relief to develop a collaboration with Action on Addiction to support the children of families with substance abuse,' explains Place2Be Chief Executive Benita Refson. 'The Duchess has a genuine interest in children's mental health and is interested in finding out more about early intervention and how to prevent long-term repercussions.' She also attended an evening reception to mark the work of the Art Room, which was held at the National Portrait Gallery. She also attended two events for the Scouts – turning makeshift baker in Cumbria when she visited a scouts camp and made sugary dough twists over the campfire, and attending the annual Scouts review at Windsor Castle.

In the countdown to her due date, there were also the usual events in the royal calendar: a Buckingham Palace garden party, Trooping the Colour and the Garter Day service, along with a church service at Westminster Abbey to celebrate the sixtieth anniversary of the Queen's coronation, which she attended with the rest of the royal family. While the Diamond Jubilee celebrations had commemorated the Queen coming to the throne, the logistics involved with planning the actual coronation ceremony took a year and so 2013 was the time to celebrate the actual coronation.

Ever since the early days of their relationship, Kate had been compared to William's mother Diana, but in the later stages of her pregnancy, she truly followed in the footsteps of the Princess of Wales and took on another royal first when she became 'godmother' to a ship. Diana had been godmother to the original Princess Cruises vessel *Royal Princess* when she launched it in 1984, but it has since been decommissioned. The new *Royal Princess* was launched by Kate on the 13 June. It was an ancient tradition, and a big honour for the godparent – in Ancient Greece, water would be poured on a vessel calling upon the gods to safeguard them at sea; in Christian tradition it became wine; breaking the bottle over the hull started in the seventeenth century; and champagne two hundred years later. It means Kate will be the godmother of the ship for life.

In her private time, Kate stopped some of the more strenuous exercise she was used to and instead started pilates classes at Hurlingham Sports and Social Club. She started knitting, and took Italian cookery classes from her new housekeeper, Antonella Fresolone. She and William were preparing to move into two new properties and so she went shopping for antiques, and also paid a visit to the nursery store Blue Almonds on Walton Street in Kensington, just around the corner from the palace. She and William spent their second wedding anniversary apart as he was serving and she was visiting Naomi House, but they spent the weekend beforehand together in Norfolk. She spent a great deal of her pregnancy in Anglesey as William was still working and so she was based there too, but she also split her time between London, Norfolk and her parents' home in Berkshire.

While there had been much debate about who would be making items for Kate's maternity wardrobe, in public she actually recycled a number of items from her pre-pregnancy wardrobe, including a dark-brown Hobbs coat that she wore in Grimsby and had previously worn to visit Alder Hey children's hospital in Liverpool; a blush-coloured coat from Joseph that she wore to the races at Cheltenham and had previously worn before she was married; a green Emilia Wickstead coat for the St Patrick's Day service that she had worn to the same ceremony the year before; and a red Armani coat that she had worn to William's passing out ceremony at Sandhurst and brought out again for her trip to Ayrshire.

Two clear maternity favourites were Emilia Wickstead – she wore a powder-blue dress for the Art Room event at the National Portrait Gallery, and a buttercup yellow coat at the Buckingham Palace garden party – and high street giant Top Shop, from which she chose a black dress with peter pan collar for her visit to Child Bereavement UK, and a black-and-white spotted number for the Harry Potter studios tour and a week later for the wedding of William van Cutsem. New labels she favoured included a Great Plains dress, and coats from Goat, Moloh and Tara Jarmon. And she didn't forgo her beloved LK Bennett nude sledges, as they were still in place along with her favourite jewellery.

In their June issue, *Vanity Fair* named her 'best dressed mum to be', and went on to explain, 'At every life stage – courtship, marriage, and now pregnancy – her classic insta-iconic pieces have inspired and influenced the wardrobes of sweethearts, brides, and mothers-to-be, respectively. The Duchess conceals her bare minimum of a bump with three-quarter length coats and skirts that also draw attention to enviably still-svelte stems.'

During her pregnancy she was also listed as one of the most influential people in the world in *Time* magazine's annual 'Time 100' list. Not only was she blooming in pregnancy, but in her royal role. In the two decades before Kate met William, she had been living her own life, and had grown to be a smart, kind, creative, self-assured and hard-working young woman. She was an individual – her own person. However, as soon as she entered the public eye she was viewed, by the press and public, only in relation to William and any time she was mentioned it was as 'Prince William's girlfriend'. It was only natural – after all, he was the one we had been looking at pictures of and reading about since he was introduced to the world on the steps of St Mary's hospital at just one day old.

However much Kate remained her own person to herself and the people who knew her, to the majority of the world she was now defined by her partner and because she didn't speak to the press, anyone could then project whatever image they wanted onto her. We are used to seeing people on our screens and in our newspapers who want to talk to the press because they need to promote a record or a political agenda. In some circumstances, something extraordinary will happen to an individual and they will share their story. However, Kate did not fall into any of those categories, and what was there to say to the press that wouldn't make her sound like she was trying to court attention?

So when she got married, it was like a second birth – her passage into public life. Now that she is living her life on a public stage and making public decisions, she can properly be discussed. She has only been in royal life for two years so it seems unfair that people are already judging her when she is still slowly and surely getting used to her position. She is comfortable in her own skin, but she is aware that she still has a lot to learn and wants to do things well, and make good and mindful decisions rather than rushing into things. Diana went from virginal nineteen-year-old nursery teacher to pregnant future queen in the space of one year and, as William stated in their engagement interview, the royal family are trying to learn from past lessons.

We are used to politicians and celebrities in the public eye and their roles are easily defined, but even though royalty has been around since long before we were born, it can still be a difficult concept to grasp in the modern world. In it are elements of the worlds of both politics and celebrity – it is a little of both and a lot of neither. The monarchy has to listen to the opinions of the public, but not necessarily act on them. They can't please everyone and shouldn't try. It is an ancient institution and many things are the same as they always have been and always will be – the role of monarch is bestowed by God, and they will not only be the figurehead of the country, but the head of the church and the military. The role is passed down through the same bloodline, and many of the traditions are still strictly adhered to.

However, the monarchy is moving through a modern age, and there have also been changes. The ancient law of primogeniture has been repealed, meaning that for the first time in history whether Kate and William's first child is male or female, he or she will take the throne after William. Other changes have seen

Prince Edward and Prince William both marry women who were of an unaristocratic background; the next in line to the throne, Prince Charles, and his wife Camilla are both divorcees; and both William and Harry went to school like all other children around the country, rather than being home-educated.

The Queen is eighty-seven years old and has been Queen for sixty-one years – in some of those years she has been unequivocally loved, in others she has been challenged. Kate herself has been criticized for not making her views known, but how much of the Queen's views do we know? She gives insights by the decisions she makes, but is actually still a remarkably private woman – she has painted a picture of herself over the years, mostly by her actions. As Kate's role is also a long-distance run, not a sprint, she may well remain something of an enigma for some time to come, and provided she has the longevity of the Queen, it will be interesting to see what is being said about her in ten years' time, or twenty, or fifty.

Kate, too, is beginning to paint a picture of herself, not with too many words at the moment, but in her actions. With her charity affiliations she has sought out vulnerable children and wretched addicts, and is encouraging others to take inspiration from the natural world, sports and the arts. She loves theatre, opera and fine art, but she is also a fan of the Harry Potter franchise, went to see *Bridesmaids* at the cinema, and by all accounts is a demon on the dance floor. She is a lady but she doesn't mind a bit of rough and tumble – always looking immaculate, painting watercolours and making jam, but she is also an outdoorsy country girl who doesn't mind getting her hair wet or her feet dirty while camping or hiking.

For her wedding day, she told her hairdresser that she wanted to look like 'herself' and when sitting for her portrait she requested that she look like her 'natural self, not her formal self'. She is proud of and dedicated to her royal position, but she doesn't allow it to totally define her – she wants to remain true to herself, and remain her own person as well, and that is what will emerge more and more over time.

Picture credits

Bibliography

Gyles Brandreth, *Charles and Camilla*, Century, 2005

Phil Dampier and Ashley Walton, *What's in the Queen's Handbag*, Book Guild, 2007

Sarah, Duchess of York, *My Story*, Simon and Schuster, 1996

Robert Jobson, *William and Kate*, John Blake, 2010

Claudia Joseph, *Kate: Kate Middleton: Princess in Waiting*, Mainstream, 2009

Penny Junor, *Prince William: Born to be King*, Hodder and Stoughton, 2012

Pippa Middleton, *Celebrate*, Michael Joseph, 2012

Andrew Morton, *Diana: Her True Story*, Michael O'Mara, 1998

Katie Nicholl, *William and Harry*, Preface, 2010

Sean Smith, *Kate*, Simon & Schuster, 2012

Acknowledgements

I very much appreciate everyone who took the time to speak to me for this book, including but not limited to Dudley Singleton, Malcolm Sutherland, Sara Johnson-Watts, Neil Swan, Tracy Rennie, Nick Barton, Sandy Nairne, Niall Scott, Benita Refson, Chris Jackson, Camilla Tominey, Jason Tait, Andy, Martin and Margot Nowell, Laura Warshauer and Michael Choong. I would also like to thank those in the Kensington Palace press office who took the time to speak to me.

Thank you to everyone who has worked hard on this book at my publishers, Michael O'Mara Books, including Louise Dixon who came to me with the idea in the first place, Toby Buchan, Judith Palmer, Ana Bjezancevic, Jessica Barrett and Ana McLaughlin. You have all been a complete delight to work with throughout the entire process. I would also like to say a big thank you for *everything* to my parents, Ralph and Joy Moody, my brother and sister-in-law, Stuart and Katherine Moody, and my grandmothers, Phyllis Moody and Joan Edwards. Thank you Annabel Chapman, David Macdonagh and Emma Gunavardhana for the feedback, and Paul Green, MDW, Oliver Grady and Catherine Morgan-Smith for all your support.

Index